Table of Contents

Philosophy and Structure

Program Objectives

Why Study Science? Science has taken its place beside language development and mathematics as one of the necessary foundations of education. Increasingly, young people need an understanding of basic scientific concepts and methods in order to assess the scientific issues that will shape their lives. It is equally important for students to have a solid grounding in the concepts and process skills used in scientific inquiry so that they will be better able to solve problems encountered in other areas of study and in dealings with the everyday world. Each *Delta Science Module* emphasizes basic science concepts and science content while developing students' process skills and increasing their appreciation for both the natural world and technology.

Why Hands-On Science? Children are fascinated by the world and enjoy opportunities to explore it. Students can best acquire science concepts and skills by means of an inquiry-based, hands-on approach that focuses on the processes and techniques of discovery. Hands-on science also helps to develop positive attitudes towards science and enhances mathematical, social, artistic, and language skills. The *Delta Science Modules* promote scientific literacy and provide opportunities for students to satisfy their innate curiosity as they develop effective techniques for observing, questioning, and testing basic scientific concepts.

Problem Solving. At the heart of the *Delta Science Modules* are the types of questions that children ask as they explore the world around them. **What will happen?** Open-ended questions encourage students to explore and begin to gather evidence. **How and why does it happen?** Students develop ideas and make inferences based on their observations while developing effective experimental techniques. **What will happen next?** Students are asked to predict, based on their observations, what will happen as the result of further experimentation. They then are encouraged to compare their results to their predictions. This, in turn, may provide the basis for more questions and additional investigations. Throughout this sequence, related content and terms are introduced.

The goal of the *Delta Science Modules* is to provide the students of today with experiences that will enable them to become scientifically literate contributors to tomorrow's society.

Components

Each *Delta Science Module* enables you to make effective and efficient use of your most valuable resource—time with your students. The components of the program are designed to provide you with the tools to help you in your role as the facilitator of learning.

Teacher's Guide. The Teacher's Guide helps to prepare you for the activities by providing a brief *Overview* of the entire module and a list of the objectives for each activity. A *Schedule of Activities* is included to help you plan ahead for your science sessions. The introduction to each module ends with *Background Information, Advance Preparation,* and *Materials Management* strategies to help you prepare for the activities. More detailed information in those three important areas is presented in the activities.

The information included in each activity provides you with a complete lesson plan. The components of each activity are described on the following page.

Objectives describe the focus and goals for the activity.

Schedule lets you know how much time to allow for the activity, and how many Sessions are necessary.

Vocabulary lists new vocabulary words introduced in the activity and defined in the Glossary.

Materials list indicates the items used in the activity, and the quantity required for each student or team.

Preparation provides detailed instructions explaining what you will need to prepare prior to beginning the activity.

Background Information explains related science content information.

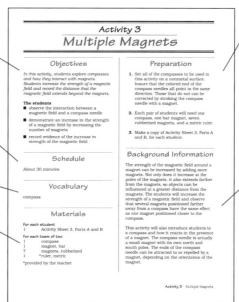

Teaching Suggestions include all of the directions for you and your students to complete the activity. The numbered steps include highlighted sample questions to assist you in leading classroom discussions.

Science at Home suggests follow-up activities that students can conduct at home.

Additional Information includes sample answers for discussion questions, tips to help you facilitate the activity, and safety reminders where appropriate.

Reinforcement provides activity suggestions for students who need more experience with the concepts presented in the activities.

Cleanup provides instructions to facilitate cleanup and the return of materials to the kit.

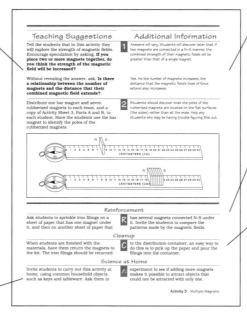

Connections at the end of each activity provide suggestions for extending and applying the concepts presented in the activity. Activities or discussion topics include *Science Challenges; Science, Technology, and Society; Science and Careers;* and subject integration in the areas of *Language Arts, Mathematics, the Arts, Social Studies,* and *Health.*

Activity Sheets. Photocopy masters for all activity sheets are included at the end of the Teacher's Guide. The activity sheets are used by students to record and interpret results, and in some cases include procedures for students to follow. You may either collect the activity sheets at the end of each activity or have students maintain a portfolio to which they may add each activity sheet as it is completed. Maintaining the activity sheets in a portfolio will enable you to review the work of each student, and also is an excellent way to provide parents with information about students' accomplishments in science. Completed activity sheets may also be used to assess a student's progress.

Performance Based Assessment. Each *Delta Science Module* Teacher's Guide includes a comprehensive assessment activity so that you may assess each student upon completion of the module. The assessment activity consists of three sections and is designed to assess each student's ability to work with materials and apply the major concepts and content introduced in the module.

Materials Kit. Each *Delta Science Module* includes almost all the materials necessary to carry out the activities with a class of 32 students. Common items and perishables are not included. Prepaid *Living Material Order Cards* are included for those modules that require live organisms. The order cards must be sent to Delta Education 4 weeks before beginning the activities that include the use of the organisms.

The materials are conveniently packaged and placed in easily accessible, durable plastic storage drawers housed in a sturdy storage module. The Materials List on page 3 of this guide indicates the quantity of each item included in the kit, and which items you will need to supply. Consumable items are indicated on this list and included in a *Refill Kit* that can be ordered from Delta Education. A convenient *Replacement Parts List* is also available so that individual items can be ordered.

Classroom Management

Materials. You may want to familiarize yourself with the kit materials before beginning the module. The contents of each drawer are listed on the drawer labels. We suggest that you refer to the Materials List on page 3 of this guide as you review the materials in each drawer.

Before beginning each activity, review the Materials list and the Preparation required for the activity. The Materials list indicates which items will be used in the activity, how many of each item will be needed for each individual and each student team, and the size of each team. We recommend that you ask student helpers to assist you in locating materials and preparing for each activity.

Distribution Stations. The most efficient way to distribute materials during an activity is to set up distribution stations from which students can obtain materials as needed. If space in your classroom is limited, you may have room for only one station. If you have more space, we recommend setting up two or three distribution stations, each containing about half or one-third of all the materials listed in the Materials list for each activity. In this way, each distribution station will contain all of the different items used in the activity, and students will not need to visit more than one station to obtain all of their materials.

Cooperative Learning. The *Delta Science Modules* encourage and promote cooperative learning strategies. The quantity of materials included in each kit allows small groups of students to investigate phenomena and each student to make observations and report what he or she has learned. The interaction between team members is an integral part of each activity and enhances individual outcomes.

Overview

This Delta Science Module introduces students to air and some of its fascinating properties; moreover, it provides hands-on experiments that enable students to see that air takes up space, has weight, exerts constantly changing pressure, and is always in motion.

Activity 1 encourages students to describe an object with which they are familiar by naming its properties. In this activity, students discover that air is indeed something, and they begin to list its properties on a class chart.

In Activity 2, students press an inverted cup full of air underwater and find that it displaces the water—the two substances are too different to mix. Students conclude that quantities of air and water cannot occupy the same space at the same time.

Students investigate the conservation of volume in Activity 3. They measure a trapped volume of air, then split the air into two parts and measure each part. They discover that the total volume is conserved—that is, it does not change.

In Activities 4 and 5, students discover two factors that can change the volume of air. In Activity 4, students alter the temperature of a bottle of air sealed with a balloon. The changing size of the balloon indicates the changing size of the volume of air inside the bottle.

In Activity 5, students gradually increase the pressure on a sealed syringe of air. They observe that the volume of air in the syringe decreases as pressure on it increases. Later, releasing the pressure, they note that the air regains its initial volume.

Activity 6 continues to dispel the myth that air is "nothing" by showing that it has weight. Students use a simple balance to compare identical balloons, one deflated

and the other inflated with air. They find the balloon full of air is heavier than the empty balloon.

The concept that air has weight prepares students for the investigation of atmospheric pressure in Activity 7. Team members construct a barometer, monitor the daily changes in its fluid level, and conclude that the air pressure on everything around us is constantly changing.

In Activity 8, students construct a setup with which they alter the air pressure inside a cup containing both water and air. They observe the effects that increasing and decreasing pressure on air can have on another material in contact with it. Students learn two important lessons in this activity: high air pressure pushes; low air pressure pulls.

In Activity 9, students discover that air slows down anything moving through it. They construct simple parachutes and experiment with them to find out how surface area affects air resistance.

The exploration of moving air continues in Activity 10, in which students assemble a simple wind speed indicator and use it to measure and record the speed of wind at various locations on the school property.

In Activity 11, students explore the Bernoulli effect. They construct a device and use it to reveal an unexpected effect of rapidly moving air: its pressure drops when it is squeezed through a narrow space.

In Activity 12, students build two types of gliders with radically different designs. They test and compare them in a contest and note the effects of different aspects of a plane's design on the way it flies.

Overview Chart

Activity	The students . . .
1 Air Is Something	• describe objects in terms of their properties • discover that air takes up space • begin to list the properties of air on a class chart
2 Air Takes Up Space	• observe that air takes up space and so can form a barrier between two other substances • infer that water and air cannot occupy the same space at the same time • discover that air can be displaced only if it has somewhere else to go
3 Air Has Volume	• observe and measure the results of dividing a volume of water • predict and observe the results of dividing a volume of air • conclude that dividing a quantity of air does not change its total volume
4 Volume Changes with Temperature	• observe and record changes in air temperature • examine the relationship between air volume and air temperature • operationally define *control*
5 Volume Changes with Pressure	• measure the volume of air in a container as the pressure on it is increased • observe the effects of pressure on a volume of air • graph their results
6 Air Has Weight	• predict whether air has weight or not • use a balance to compare weights of inflated and deflated balloons • determine that air has weight
7 Air Exerts Pressure	• infer that because air has weight, it must exert pressure • build a barometer to measure air pressure • monitor the changes in air pressure over the course of a week • conclude that air pressure is constantly changing
8 High Pressure— Low Pressure	• observe that pushing or pulling on air causes it to push or pull on water in contact with it • recall that increased pressure on air decreased its volume and infer that the inverse must also be true • conclude that high air pressure pushes and low air pressure pulls
9 Air Resistance	• observe the effects of air resistance on falling objects • infer that the larger the area of an object, the greater the air resistance to its movement • discover that the faster an object moves, the greater the air resistance to its movement
10 Air Moves	• discuss evidence that air moves • make instruments to measure wind speed • measure and record wind speed data and discuss possible reasons for differences in wind speed
11 The Bernoulli Effect	• construct a device that indicates a pressure drop in a fast-moving stream of air • observe that two foam balls move toward one another as air flows between them • operationally define the *Bernoulli effect*
12 Paper Airplanes	• make and test two glider designs for performance • discuss the variables that affect a glider's flight • modify their glider designs to try to improve their performance

Materials List

Qty		Description
1		bag, plastic, reclosable, 15 cm × 15 cm
16	c	bags, plastic, 30-gallon
1	c	bags, plastic, with ties, p/35
3	c	balloons, large, p/12
25	c	balloons, small
16		balls, foam
8		bases, foam, for syringes
8		bases, balance
8		beams, balance
9		bottles, plastic
8	c	cardboard, corrugated
1	c	chart, Barometer Data
1	c	chart, Pressure Graph
1	c	chart, Properties of Air
1	c	clay, modeling, 0.25 lb
8		containers, plastic, 6-L
8	c	cups, paper, 10-oz
16		cups, plastic, 10-oz
16		cylinders, graduated, 50-cc
1		Daily Air Pressure
1		Dart Design
2	c	dots, adhesive, blue, p/28
16		eyes, plastic
1	c	food coloring, red, 1 oz
8		measuring tapes
1		paper clips, large, p/100
1	c	paper clips, small, p/100
8		pins, balance
1		rubber bands, p/200
8		rubber stoppers, with hole
1		Slider Design
1	c	string, 75-m
8		syringes

Qty		Description
1	c	tape, duct
1	c	tape, masking
9		thermometers, Celsius
1		transparency, Graduated Cylinder
8		trapezoid pieces
4		tubing, thick, 20-cm, p/4
1		tubing, thin, 50-cm, p/8
32		washers, metal
8		Wind Speed Indicator cards
1		teacher's guide

Teacher provided items

Qty	Description
8	bottles, glass, narrow-necked
1	clock or watch, with second hand
8	containers, 2-L or greater
32	crayons
1	funnel
–	ice cubes
1	knife, dull
1	marker, erasable
1	marker, felt-tip
–	newspaper
1	overhead projector
–	paper towels
–	paper, plain
32	pencils
1	pitcher
1	ruler, metric
1	scissors
1	spoon, stirring
–	tape, transparent
32	textbooks
–	water, tap

c = consumable item

Schedule of Activities

Activity Number and Title	Session 1	2	3	4	5	6	7	8	9	10	11	12	13	14	15	16
1 Air Is Something	■															
2 Air Takes Up Space		■														
3 Air Has Volume		●	■													
4 Volume Changes with Temperature			●	■												
5 Volume Changes with Pressure				●	■											
6 Air Has Weight						■										
7 Air Exerts Pressure						●		■								
8 High Pressure—Low Pressure									■							
9 Air Resistance									●		■					
10 Air Moves											●	■				
11 The Bernoulli Effect													■			
12 Paper Airplanes													●		■	
Assessment																■

➤ Continuing observation or wait time required ● Advance preparation required

Preparing for the Activities

Background Information

We are in contact with air every moment of our lives. We need air to breathe, to fly our airplanes, and to inflate our tires. Yet most of the time we are completely unaware of the air around us because it has no color, taste, or odor. We even think of a cup of air as being empty.

Even when we are aware of air, it is easy to take it for granted. But it is important to realize what a truly amazing substance it is. It extends for a hundred miles above us, and is capable of moving at speeds up to hundreds of miles per hour. It shields our planet and ourselves from harmful rays from the Sun. It provides the oxygen our bodies need to perform metabolic functions. Our very existence depends on air.

This module is designed to introduce students to the concept of air as "something," possessing properties that can be perceived and measured, like those of any other material. Students learn that air can be felt, weighed, moved around, compressed, expanded, heated, and cooled. At the same time, they become aware of the many ways we use it—in the simple, but vital, act of breathing as well as in the more complex task of flying an airplane.

The air around us is a mixture of many gases, such as oxygen, argon, and carbon dioxide, but it is mostly nitrogen. It exhibits one basic property of essentially all gases: it is invisible, requiring students to observe its effects on other substances in order to discover its properties. By trapping air inside containers, they can more easily feel it, measure it, and manipulate it.

The most notable property of contained air is its volume. Although under stable conditions the volume of air does not change, some factors do lead to a change in the volume of air. Heating air increases its volume, as does decreasing any external pressure on it. Cooling or compressing air has the opposite effect on its volume.

Like any other substance, air has mass, and therefore weight. (Although we are actually talking about the mass of air, we use the more familiar term *weight* in these activities.) Although it is much lighter than any solid or liquid, the weight of all the air above and around us in the atmosphere is tremendous; it presses down with a force of 10 tons on every square meter!

Air also pushes on air. Uneven heating of air over different areas of land and water results in differences in air pressure over those areas. The more the air is heated, the more its pressure decreases, and the more it tends to rise. Cooler, higher-pressure air then flows in around and beneath it, creating the winds that move constantly over the face of the planet.

Like every other substance, air is made up of molecules. Any object moving through air collides with those molecules. The larger the object and the greater its speed, the more molecules it must push aside simultaneously. While air resistance against the movement of small objects at low speeds may be trivial, it can become significant in, for example, slowing the descent of a parachutist or limiting the speed at which a car or plane can travel.

One of the most interesting effects of fast-moving air is the Bernoulli effect, named after a Swiss scientist who studied air movement. He noted that as air speeds up, its pressure drops. Among other practical applications, the effect is responsible for creating much of the "lift"—the pressure differential above and below a fast-moving wing—that permits airplanes, birds, and insects to fly.

The Bernoulli effect is a major consideration in the design of an airplane. The stream of air over the curved upper surface of the wing moves faster than that over the lower, flatter surface; as its pressure drops, it lifts the wing.

An understanding of the properties of air enriches students' appreciation of the world around them, whether they are flying a kite, watching a tree bend in the wind, turning on a fan, or blowing out the candles on their birthday cake.

Advance Preparation

Prior to Activity 1, decide on the best place to post the Properties of Air chart in the classroom so that the whole class can easily see and refer to it throughout the module. Also, decide on an object to ask students to describe. A good choice would be an object that appeals to their physical senses—one with strong color, distinctive texture, definite shape, and even a odor or taste with which they are familiar.

Reserve or set aside an overhead projector and an erasable marker for use in Activity 3. The manipulation of tubing, syringe, and cylinders underwater in the experiment is a two- or three-handed operation; you may want to solicit the help of a couple of students (or other volunteers) to do a trial run before you conduct the activity.

You will need to provide ice cubes, hot tap water, and cold tap water for Activity 4 and the assessment activity. In addition, you will need a clock or watch with a second hand in Activity 4.

Collect at least 32 hardcover textbooks of relatively uniform size and weight for use in Activity 5. You may want to prepare the sealed syringes (see Preparation in Activity 5) in advance, as well, since they may require extra time for proper assembly.

For the barometers in Activity 7, you will need to collect eight glass bottles. Clear, narrow-necked glass bottles with a capacity of at least 20 ounces will work well. (Plastic bottles are not suitable for these barometers.) Clean the bottles and soak off any labels. Be sure to check to see that the black rubber stopper included in the kit fits snugly in the neck of each bottle. Also, decide on a place in the classroom to set up eight barometers where they can remain for a week of continuing observation. They should be kept out of direct sunlight and away from the effects of any heating or cooling unit.

In Activity 9, students test wind resistance by running with their parachutes. Arrange for the use of a large, open space indoors, such as the gym. Alternatively, a long, empty hall will do.

For the wind-speed measurements in Activity 10, you will need to take the class outside. In advance of the activity, check the weather report and investigate a variety of locations where students would usually find both high and low wind speeds. You may want to have parent volunteers or older students assist you in supervising student groups around the school yard.

Activity 12 requires a large, open space for flying paper airplanes. Calm air is best for this flight contest, so try to reserve an indoor space, such as the gym or cafeteria. A stopwatch is ideal for timing the flights, but a watch with a second hand will do.

Materials Management

Several activities call for tap water, both hot and cold. If there is no sink in the classroom, you may want to use pitchers to transport water for the activities. Whenever water is on the list of materials for an activity, it is a good idea to provide newspapers with which students can cover their work areas. Plan to have a mop, sponges, and extra paper towels handy in case of spills.

Activity 1
Air Is Something

Objectives

Students learn that air is not "nothing" but is a substance with physical properties.

The students
- describe objects in terms of their properties
- discover that air takes up space
- begin to list the properties of air on a class chart

Schedule

About 40 minutes

Vocabulary

air
properties

Materials

For each student
1	Activity Sheet 1, Parts A and B
1	bag, plastic, with tie
1	*crayon, any color

For each team of four
1	balloon, small
1	syringe

For the class
1	bag, plastic, with tie
1	chart, Properties of Air
1	*marker, felt-tip
4 pc	tubing, plastic, thin, 50-cm

*provided by the teacher

Preparation

1. Make a copy of Activity Sheet 1, Parts A and B, for each student.

2. Remove and set aside the protective caps from the tips of the syringes before you distribute them.

3. Use tape or pins to attach the Properties of Air chart to the board or a wall where all students can see it. You may want to leave a felt-tip marker next to the chart for later use.

4. Decide on a familiar object students can describe at the beginning of the activity in order to grasp the concept of *properties*. An object that can be seen, felt, heard, or smelled would serve the purpose best.

5. Each student will need a plastic bag with tie and a crayon. Each team of four will need a small balloon and a syringe.

Background Information

Young students often have difficulty recognizing that air is a substance. This is because it eludes their primary senses: it is invisible, odorless, and except as wind, cannot really be felt.

During the course of the module, students will be asked to describe the properties of air. In order to prepare them for describing such an intangible substance, it is helpful to first encourage them to describe the properties of objects they easily perceive. Good choices are objects that appeal to their physical senses—objects with strong color, distinctive texture, definite shape, and even a discernible odor or taste, if possible. Such objects will elicit the longest list of descriptive words and phrases.

Such an exercise serves to help students think of an object as a sum of its properties. The more properties of a substance students can name, the better understanding they will have of that substance. As students discover the many properties of air over the course of these activities, they begin to get a picture of what sort of substance it really is.

In this first activity, students experiment with a variety of instruments that focus their attention on the presence of air. In each of these experiments, they observe evidence that air exists. They also begin to identify some of the properties of air.

First, students blow into a bag and seal it off. The inflated bag resists being pressed on and has a shape. Thus, they see that air is a substance that takes up space. Second, by pushing air through a syringe, they are able to feel it as wind. They further explore the movement of air in several ways, from blowing it from their mouths to fanning with their hands. Lastly, by connecting two syringes with a piece of rubber tubing, they are able to see that air pushed out of one syringe will push back the plunger of the other syringe. The lesson in this activity is that air takes up space, and, when pushed on, will in turn push on something else.

Name _____ Activity Sheet 1, Part A

Air Is Something

1. Blow up your plastic bag until it is full and tie it shut.

What is inside the bag? <u>air</u>

2. In the pictures below, draw the balloon as it looked on the end of the syringe with the plunger pushed in; then draw it as it looked with the plunger pulled out.

3. In each picture above, color the place where air is.

Did the air move when you pulled back the plunger to the end of the syringe? If so, where did it come from, and where did it go?

<u>Yes, it moved. It moved from inside the balloon to inside the syringe.</u>

Name _____ Activity Sheet 1, Part B

Air Is Something

4. With your teammates, connect the two syringes with the piece of tubing, as shown below.

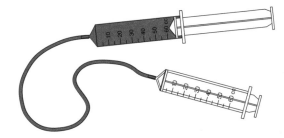

5. In the picture above, color in the place where air is.

What happened when you pushed in the plunger of one syringe?

<u>The second plunger moved out.</u>

Why did the second plunger move out in its syringe when you pushed in the plunger of the first syringe?

<u>The air in the first syringe moved into the tubing and into the second syringe, where it pressed on the plunger and moved it out.</u>

Teaching Suggestions	Additional Information

1

Hold up a familiar object, such as a piece of fruit, a ruler, a marshmallow, or a sheet of construction paper—whatever you have chosen to exhibit—in front of the students and ask, **What is the name of this object?**

Students should call out the name of the object.

Ask, **Now that you have named this object, what words can you think of that would describe it?**

If necessary, elicit responses by asking students questions about the object's color, texture, shape, odor, and so forth.

Make a list of students' descriptions on the board. Tell students that the words they use to describe an object are called its *properties.* Write the word above the list on the board and underline it.

Ask them to name some properties of any object they can think of, indoors or out, to confirm that they understand what is meant by a *property* of something.

Students may describe such things as a piece of clothing, a rock, a tree, rain, clouds, and so on.

2

Write *air* on the board. Ask, **What is air?**

Answers will vary, but most students will probably say that air is the stuff all around us that we breathe.

Ask, **Can you think of any properties of air?**

Accept all reasonable responses. Write them on the board and allow for discussion.

Tell students that in the following activities they will be doing experiments to find out whether air has properties and, if so, what they are. Point out the chart, Properties of Air, and tell them that every time they discover a new property, you will add it to the chart.

3

Give each student a copy of Activity Sheet 1, Part A, an empty plastic bag with a tie, and a crayon. Ask, **Is there anything inside the bag?**

Students will probably say that the bag is empty.

Next, take a plastic bag and demonstrate how to inflate it by blowing into it. Show students how to twist the open end closed and tie it tightly. Ask students to do the same with their plastic bags. When all students have done so, ask, **Is your bag still empty? What is now inside?**

Students will probably say that the bag is no longer empty because their breath is in the bag.

Explain that their breath is air, like the air around them in the classroom. Have students answer the first question on Part A of their activity sheets.

Have students feel their bag of air. Ask, **Why is the bag no longer flat? Why does it take up more space than it did before?**

Encourage students to conclude that the bag is no longer flat because the air inside it takes up space.

Ask students to hold up their bags and show each other how much space their air takes up.

Point out that they have just identified a property of air and write *Air takes up space* on the Properties of Air chart. Tell students that next they will do another experiment that shows how air takes up space.

Distribute a small balloon and a syringe to each team of four.

4

Borrow a syringe from one of the teams and show the class how to pull back on the plunger and then push it in.

Tell students when they are told to pull the plunger outward, they should pull it back only until it stops at the end of the syringe. Caution them not to remove the plunger from the syringe because that might damage it.

Have one student from each team take the syringe and pull back the plunger. Then, while pointing the tip down, a few inches from a second student's hand, have him or her quickly push in the plunger. Ask the second students what they felt on their hands.

Students should say that they felt wind, or moving air.

Ask, **What made the air move out of the syringe?**

Students should suggest that the plunger pushed the air out of the syringe.

Point out to students that by pushing on air, they can create wind. Lead them to conclude that wind is just moving air. Discuss with students how, although we cannot see air, we can feel it when it moves against our skin.

Allow each student in the team to take a turn blowing on a teammate's hand with the syringe. Then ask, **Can you make air move by using your bodies instead of a syringe?**

Students may fan air with their hands or blow it from their mouths. Ask them if they can feel their stomachs pressing the air out when they blow, as the plunger pressed the air out of the syringe.

Tell one student from each team to pull out the syringe's plunger again. Have another student fit the balloon over the end without pressing in the plunger. Then have a third student press in the plunger while the others watch. Ask, **What happened?**

Students should point out that the balloon filled up with air.

Ask, **Where did the air that filled up the balloon come from?**

It came from inside the syringe.

Have the fourth student in each team pull the balloon off the end of the syringe, press the plunger in and put the balloon back on the end. Ask, **What do you think will happen if you pull the plunger out?**

Accept all reasonable answers.

Have each team pass the syringe back to the first student and let him or her pull out the plunger.

Ask, **What happened?**

The balloon collapsed.

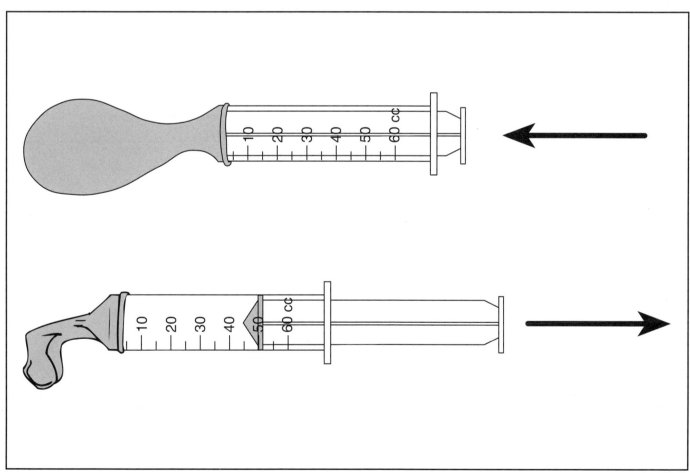

Figure 1-1. Pushing in the plunger on the syringe fills the balloon with air. Pulling outward on the plunger removes the air and collapses the balloon.

Lead students to conclude that in order for the balloon to have collapsed the air must have gone out of it. Ask, **Where do you think the air went?**

Students may say that the air that was inside the balloon was pulled into the syringe.

Ask students to complete Part A of the activity sheet.

7

Have teams pair up to make teams of eight students each and give each team a 50-cm piece of tubing. Give each student a copy of Activity Sheet 1, Part B, and ask all the students to take a few moments to study the illustration in Step 4 before proceeding with the next experiment.

Tell students they will now take turns assembling the setup shown on the activity sheet. Ask one student in each group to pick up a syringe and press the plunger all the way in. Ask another student to take the other syringe and pull the plunger back to the end. Then have a third student push the tubing onto the tip of one syringe and a fourth student attach the free end of the tubing to the tip of the other syringe.

Students may find it difficult to fit the tubing over the tip of the syringe. Offer help as needed.

Allow a fifth student to press in the plunger of the open syringe and ask students to describe what happened.

The other plunger was pushed outward in its syringe.

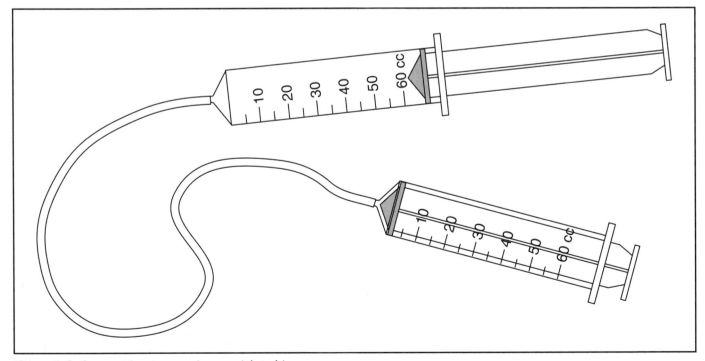

Figure 1-2. Connecting two syringes with tubing.

When each team member has had a chance to push in the plunger of one of the syringes, ask, **When you pushed in the plunger on one syringe, what made the plunger on the second syringe move outward?**

Students should say that air pushed it outward.

Lead students to conclude that when the first plunger was pressed in, it forced the air out of the first syringe, through the tubing, and into the second syringe, where it pressed against the plunger and moved it outward in the syringe.

Ask, **If air did not take up space, would the second plunger have moved outward?**

Students should conclude that it would not.

Have students complete Part B of their activity sheets.

Tell students they have discovered one of the properties of air (that it takes up space). Tell them they will discover even more properties in the following activities.

Reinforcement

Make a list of examples students can offer of objects they are familiar with in which air takes up space. It may be helpful to phrase the question thus: **How many objects can** **you think of that are useful because they have air inside them?** Students might mention various kinds of balls, tires, or even blimps.

Cleanup

Dispose of the plastic bags and ties. Have students disconnect the tubing from the syringes. Replace the protective caps on the tips of the syringes and return them, along with the tubing and balloons, to the kit. Leave the Properties of Air chart posted throughout all the following activities.

Science at Home

Ask students to look for inflatable toys and other items at home. Tell them to notice the difference in the amount of space they take up when they are full of air (inflated) and when they are empty of air (deflated).

Connections

Science Extension

To give students additional practice describing the properties of objects, play a game of "I Spy." Model the procedure by choosing an object without revealing what it is and describing its properties—"I spy something long, thin, hard, yellow, and pointed on one end," for a pencil, for example—and let students guess the object. Once they have the idea, let them take turns choosing and describing objects.

Do the following activity as a demonstration. Put a clear plastic funnel into the top of a clear jar and mold clay around the jar's rim, making sure there are no holes or gaps. Show students the jar and ask them whether there is anything in it. (They will probably say no.) Pour tinted water into the funnel. (The water will stay in the funnel.) Then poke a small hole through the clay. The water will flow from the funnel into the jar. Ask students to explain this observation. (The jar was not empty but was filled with air. The water could not flow into the jar while there was air in it, but when you made a hole in the clay, the air was pushed out of the jar and the water flowed in.)

Science and Careers

Invite a professional or hobbyist clown who entertains at children's parties to visit the class and show students how to make animals with inflated balloons. (Look in the Yellow Pages under the heading *Clowns*.) Ask the visitor to demonstrate the air pump or oxygen tank used to inflate the balloons and to describe how it works. Provide an ample supply of balloons so students can try their hand at making balloon creatures. Also ask the visitor to explain how he or she learned to be a clown and what is involved in creating a unique clown character.

Science and Language Arts

Provide library books about air to read aloud to small groups or to make available for students to read on their own if they are capable. Three good choices are described below.

Air by David Bennett (Bantam, 1989): Easy-to-read text and simple illustrations make this book appropriate for younger readers; covers many aspects of air in simple terms.

Air by David Lloyd (Dial, 1982): Text is appropriate for mature readers, but the dramatic and captivating illustrations by Peter Visscher could simply be used as a basis for discussion with beginning readers.

The Air I Breathe by Bobbie Kalman and Janine Schaub (Crabtree, 1993): For more capable readers; covers a wider range of topics and more detail than the Bennett book described above.

Science, Technology, and Society

Let students use a bicycle pump to blow puffs of air at their hands or at objects that will move when air hits them. If you can trust students not to blow up balloons to the point of bursting (or if you do not mind the noise of popping balloons), let students attach a balloon to the end of the tube and blow it up. Ask students whether the pump pulls air back out of the balloon when they pull the plunger back. (No; the pump draws air through a separate intake hole, so it does not pull air from the balloon or from a tire being inflated.) Save the pump for use again in Science, Technology, and Society for Activities 5 and 8.

Activity 2
Air Takes Up Space

Objectives

Students further confirm the fact that air takes up space when they observe the displacement both of water by air and of air by water.

The students

■ observe that air takes up space and so can form a barrier between two other substances

■ infer that water and air cannot occupy the same space at the same time

■ discover that air can be displaced only if it has somewhere else to go

Schedule

About 40 minutes

Vocabulary

displace
prediction

Materials

For each student
1   Activity Sheet 2, Parts A and B

For each team of four
1   cup, paper, 10-oz
1   cup, plastic, 10-oz
2   *paper towels
1   syringe
1 pc   tubing, plastic, thin, 50-cm

For the class
1   *chart, Properties of Air (from Activity 1)
8   containers, plastic, 6-L
1 btl   food coloring, red
1   *marker, felt-tip
           *newspapers
           *paper towels
1   *spoon, stirring
1 roll   tape, masking
           *water, tap

*provided by the teacher

Preparation

1. Make a copy of Activity Sheet 2, Parts A and B, for each student.

2. Fill each 6-L plastic container three-quarters-full with tap water (up to about 5 cm below the rim). Stir a few drops of red food coloring into each container. (The red tint will allow students to distinguish between the air and the water.)

3. Remove and set aside the protective caps from the tips of the syringes before you distribute them.

4. Tear off eight 5-cm (about 2-in.) pieces of masking tape from the roll.

5. Keep extra paper towels on hand to clean up any spills.

6. Each team will need a container of colored water, a paper cup, a plastic cup, two paper towels, a syringe, and a piece of tubing.

Background Information

A quantity of air in a container occupies the space just as fully as a quantity of sand, water, or anything else. Because air takes up space, it can act as a barrier between two substances on either side of it. If a cup of air is overturned and lowered under water, the pocket of air trapped inside acts as a barrier between the top of the cup and the water (see Figure 2-1).

While the cup is inverted, the air and water inside will remain completely separate; different materials generally do not mix unless they have very similar properties. The great difference between the densities of air and water prevent the two substances from sharing a common space.

The second part of this activity builds on the idea that air takes up space by introducing students to the concept of *displacement*. Because air and water both take up space and cannot occupy the same space at the same time, either one can be made to displace the other.

For example, when air is blown into an inverted cup full of water, the air collects at the top of the cup and displaces the water that is there, pushing it down and out of the cup. In this instance, water is displaced by air. However, if a hole is cut in the bottom of that cup, and the cup of air is inverted and pushed down into the water again, the air exits through this hole, and water moves in to fill the vacated space. In this instance, air is displaced by water.

In this activity, students witness the displacement first of water by air and then of air by water.

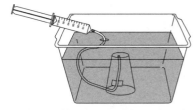

Teaching Suggestions	Additional Information

Teaching Suggestions

Give each student a copy of Activity Sheet 2, Parts A and B. To each team of four, distribute a 6-L container of colored water, one paper cup, one plastic cup, two paper towels, a syringe, and a 50-cm piece of thin plastic tubing.

Hold up one team's empty paper cup and ask, **Is there anything inside this cup?**

Have one student on each team hold the paper cup while a second student gently crumples a paper towel and tucks it into the bottom of the cup. Hold up one team's cup and show students that the paper towel must fit in the bottom third of the cup so that it does not fall out when the cup is turned upside down.

Tell students that when you tell them to do so—but not immediately—a third student on each team will hold the cup upside down and press it straight down to the bottom of the container of water and hold it there until you say to lift it out.

First, write *prediction* on the board and ask, **What do you think a *prediction* is?**

Explain that a prediction is a guess based on previous experience about what will probably happen in a certain situation. Tell students that scientists always try to predict what the results of their experiments will be, but their predictions are not always correct. Assure students that it does not mean they are wrong if their predictions do not turn out to be true.

Ask students to predict whether the paper towel will be wet or dry when it is removed from the container. Have them record their predictions on Part A of the activity sheet.

Additional Information

1 Have teams cover their work areas with newspaper to soak up any spills. Show them where to get extra paper towels if they need them.

Answers will vary. Some students may say the cup is empty, but most will recall from the previous activity that because air is all around, there must be air in the cup. Encourage students to reach consensus that the cup is full of air.

2

Answers will vary. Some students may know that a prediction is a guess about something that will happen,

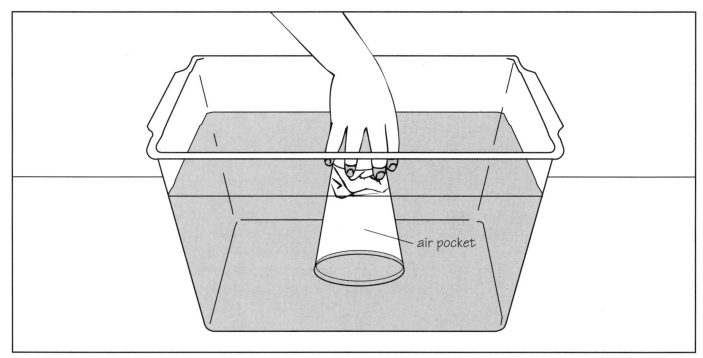

air pocket

Figure 2-1. A cross section of the paper cup and towel under water.

When they have done so, tell the third student on each team to hold the cup upside down and, without tipping it to one side or another, press it straight down to the bottom of the container of water and hold it there until you say to lift it out. Then tell the student holding the cup in the water to lift it straight up out of the water and hand it, still upside down, to the fourth student on the team. Have the student remove the crumpled paper towel and pass it around to the other members of the team. Ask, **What do you observe about the towel?**

The towel is dry.

Have students record this observation on their activity sheets.

Ask, **Did you predict that the towel would be dry?**

Most students will probably answer no.

Ask, **Why do you think the towel stayed dry?**

Students may suggest that the air in the cup kept the water away from the paper towel.

Remind students that they learned in Activity 1 that air takes up space. Explain that the air in the inverted cup took up space between the water under the cup and the paper towel. Thus, it acted as a barrier between the two and kept the towel from getting wet.

Tell students they will next construct the setup shown in Step 3 on Part B of Activity Sheet 2. Instruct each team to first stick one end of the plastic tubing into the plastic cup until it touches the bottom. Walk around and give each team a 5-cm piece of masking tape and show them how to use it to hold the tubing in place inside the cup. Direct one student from each team to attach the other end of the tubing to the syringe. Then have a second student pull the plunger out to the end of the syringe.

Students may find it difficult to fit the tubing over the tip of the syringe. Offer help as needed.

Have a third student on each team place the plastic cup sideways into the container of water so that it fills completely with water. Then tell that student to flip the cup upside down and hold it near the bottom.

Ask all students to predict what will happen when they push in the plunger and have them write their predictions on Part B of the activity sheet. When they have finished, have the fourth student in each group slowly press in the plunger while the team members watch the cup. Ask, **What is happening?**

The top of the cup is filling with air.

Have students record their observations on Part B of their activity sheets.

Have students describe what just happened. Ask, **What is in the top of the cup? Where did it come from? How did it get there? What did it do to the water?**

Air is now in the top of the cup. It came from inside the syringe, moved through the tubing, and pushed the water out of the cup.

Ask, **Can air and water can be in the same space at the same time?**

No, only one or the other can occupy a space.

Write *displace* on the board and tell students that when one substance forces another out of the way, it is said to displace that substance. Ask, **In your cup, did the water displace the air, or did the air displace the water?**

The air displaced the water.

Remind students that air takes up space and so can move things when pushed into them.

Have students recall how, in Activity 1, the air pushed through the tubing by the plunger of one syringe moved out the plunger of the other syringe.

Ask, **Where did the water in the cup go when it was displaced by the air?**

It went out of the cup and back into the container.

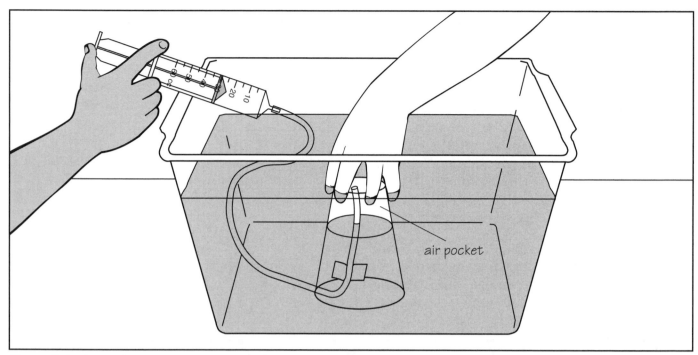

Figure 2-2. Using the syringe to create a pocket of air in the cup.

 7

Have each team take their cup out of the water and remove the syringe from the end of the tubing. Then have one student on each team hold his or her finger tightly over the end of the tubing while another student pushes the cup, upside down, to the bottom of the container. Have them hold both in position until you say to move them. Ask, **What happened this time?**

Air is still inside the cup.

Ask, **What do you think will happen if the end of the tubing is opened?** Have them write their predictions down in Step 4 of Part B of their activity sheets. As soon as they have done so, ask all students to be very quiet and listen carefully as the team members remove their fingers from the ends of the pieces of tubing.

Answers will vary.

Students holding the materials will not be able to write down their predictions themselves.

Students should hear a hiss of air as the water fills up the cup and the air rushes out of the tubing.

Ask students to record what happened on their activity sheets.

Ask, **What happened when the air escaped from the cup?**

The water moved in and displaced the air.

Ask, **Can water displace air if the air cannot escape?**

No, air has to have somewhere to go for water to displace it.

Have students answer the last question on Part B of the activity sheet.

Walk from team to team and use a pencil or pen to poke a hole in the bottom of each paper cup. Ask, **What do you think will happen if you lower a crumpled paper towel in a cup with a hole in it?**

Tell students to go back to the bottom half of Part A of the activity sheet to record their predictions.

Have teams perform the experiment and then remove the paper towels and examine them. Ask, **Are your paper towels dry?**

Students will find that the paper towels are soaked.

Have them record their observations. Then ask, **Why did the paper towel get wet this time?**

The air could escape through the hole, so the water displaced it and got the towel wet.

Have students record their explanations, completing the activity sheet.

Ask students to review what happened to the paper towel in the two experiments. Steer the conversation until the following becomes clear:

1. The first time, the air could not escape because there was no hole in the cup.

2. Since the air could not escape, water could not displace the air, and the towel stayed dry.

3. The second time, the air could escape through the hole in the cup.

4. Since the air could escape, the water displaced the air, and the towel got wet.

Call students' attention to the Properties of Air chart. Ask, **Did your observations in this activity confirm that the first property of air we listed in the chart is true?**

Students should all say yes, air takes up space.

Reinforcement

Have students repeat the experiment with the crumpled paper towel in the paper cup with a hole in the bottom. This time, tell each to hold one hand a little way above the hole as they lower the cup into the water and try to feel the air escaping from the cup.

Cleanup

Discard the paper cups and the masking tape strips from the plastic cups. Rinse and air-dry the large plastic containers, plastic cups, pieces of tubing, and syringes; return them (after replacing the caps on the syringes) along with the masking tape and food coloring to the kit.

Connections

Science Challenge

Set up a learning station with a water-filled aquarium and two clear cups. Challenge teams to figure out a way to "pour" air from one cup to the other with both cups held under water. (Push one cup into the water upside-down so it stays full of air, and turn the other cup sideways as it is lowered so it fills with water. Hold both cups upside-down and close together, with the water-filled cup a bit higher than the air-filled cup. Tilt the air-filled cup so bubbles escape and rise into the other cup.)

Use the following activities to show students that air takes up space within other materials.

Air in soil. Provide (or ask students to collect) soil samples from the school yard or areas around their homes. (Do not use samples that are primarily clay soil.) Have each team fill a clear jar about halfway with water and then add a cupful of soil. Students will see bubbles of air escaping from the soil and rising through the water to its surface. Explain that all soil has some air in it, in spaces between the bits of dirt and pebbles.

Air in water. Have each team fill a clear jar with cold water and look at the water through the side of the jar. (No air bubbles will be visible.) Then tell students to put the jar in a sunny place and leave it there for a few hours. When students look at the jar again, they will see tiny air bubbles clinging to the side. Explain that water has air in it. When cold water is warmed, the air forms tiny bubbles.

Science Extension

Let each student blow up a plastic or paper bag and then seal it shut with tape or a rubber band. Tell students to put the bag down and place a book on top of it. What happens? (The book rests on the bag without flattening it.) What is holding the book up? (the air inside the bag) What happens if they open the bag or poke a hole in it? (The weight of the book forces air out of the bag, and it flattens.)

Have each team crumple a small piece of paper into a ball and float it on top of the water in a bowl. Tell them to hold a clear plastic cup upside down over the paper ball and push the cup straight down into the water. Students will see that the cup stays full of air and the paper ball still floats on the lowered water surface below the cup.) Ask students to explain this observation. (The air in the cup pushes the water down so it cannot enter the cup.)

Science and the Arts

Ask students whether they have ever seen gymnasts or people in parades using wands with strips of colored fabric attached to make circles and swirls in the air. Suggest that students make their own "color wands" by taping long strips of crepe paper to a dowel or ruler. Take the class outdoors or to a gym or other large, open, indoor area so students can experiment with making swirls.

Science and Health

Bring in two or three child-size life vests used by boaters, and let students try them on. Explain that the vests have air inside. Air is lighter than water, so the vest floats and holds up the person wearing it. Stress that everyone, even strong swimmers, should wear a life vest when boating or water skiing, and discuss the reasons for this safety precaution. (Someone who falls into the water in a boating accident might be injured and unable to swim, or the water might be too rough for even a strong swimmer.)

Activity 3
Air Has Volume

Objectives

Students discover that the volume of a trapped quantity of air is conserved if split in two.

The students

■ observe and measure the results of dividing a volume of water

■ predict and observe the results of dividing a volume of air

■ conclude that dividing a quantity of air does not change its total volume

Schedule

About 50 minutes

Vocabulary

conserved
cubic centimeter (cc)
graduated cylinder
volume

Materials

For each student
1   Activity Sheet 3, Parts A and B

For each team of four
2   cylinders, graduated, 50-cc
1   syringe

For the class
1   *chart, Properties of Air (from Activity 2)
8   containers, plastic, 6-L

1 btl   food coloring, red
1   *marker, erasable
1   *marker, felt-tip
             *newspaper
1   *overhead projector
             *paper towels
1   *ruler, metric
1   *spoon, stirring
1 roll   tape, masking
1   transparency, Graduated Cylinder
8 pc   tubing, plastic, thin, 50-cm
             *water, tap

*provided by the teacher

Preparation

1. Make a copy of Activity Sheet 3, Parts A and B, for each student.

2. Make sure to reserve an overhead projector for use at the beginning of class. Leave the transparency on top of the glass plate along with the erasable marker.

3. Fill each 6-L plastic container three-quarters-full with tap water (up to about 5 cm below the rim). Stir a few drops of red food coloring into each container.

4. Remove and set aside the caps from the tips of the syringes before distributing them.

5. For each team, prepare a length of tubing as shown in Figure 3-1: Take one 50-cm (about 20-in.) length of tubing and bend it into a fishhook shape so that one side is about 12 cm (about 4.8 in.) longer than the other. Cut a 10-cm (about 4-in.) piece of

masking tape and place it 5 cm (about 2 in.) up from the bottom of the loop, wrapping it around both sides of the loop to hold them about 6 cm apart. The shorter end of the tubing above the masking tape should measure about 13 cm (about 5.2 in.) so that it will extend all the way to the top of the graduated cylinder when placed inside it.

6. Each team will need a container of colored water, two graduated cylinders, a syringe, and a prepared hook-shaped piece of tubing.

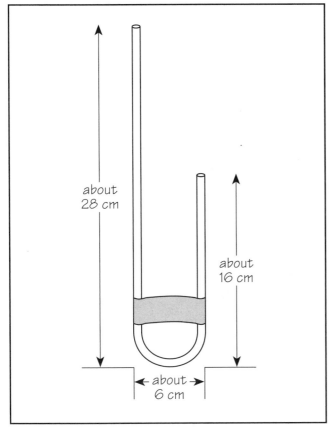

about
28 cm

about
16 cm

← about →
6 cm

Figure 3-1. *A taped piece of thin plastic tubing.*

Background Information

Air, like any substance, is composed of molecules. The molecules are in constant motion and will spread out to fill any container they occupy. For this reason, air can be said to have no definite *volume.*

However, if air is forced into a confined space, such as a bag or the top of an inverted flask, so that the container can hold no more molecules (at that temperature and pressure), that quantity of air can be said to have a certain volume.

If that quantity of air is split into two parts, its volume is *conserved;* that is, the sum of the two smaller quantities is equal to the original larger quantity. The fundamental principle of this activity then is very simple: when a body of trapped air is divided into different containers, its total volume remains the same. (Students will most likely be familiar with the conservation of volume for liquids and solids, as they have inevitably had to divide a muffin or a glass of milk in two to share with a friend.) This is a valuable lesson for students because in later activities they will experiment with a quantity of air to see if they can change its volume. Having seen the results of this activity, however, they will be able to correctly conclude that no matter what the volume, the total is not changed by dividing it into smaller quantities.

The concept of *conservation* is an important tool for all kinds of scientific exploration. This activity introduces the idea by demonstrating the conservation of volume. Students also have the opportunity to use math—in this case, addition—to confirm their observations.

Name _____ Activity Sheet 3, Part A

Air Has Volume

Before Pouring:

1. In the picture, color the space where water is.

   What is the volume of water in the first cylinder?

   _50 cc_

   In the second cylinder?

   _0 cc_

   What is the total volume of water in the first and second cylinders?

   _50 cc_

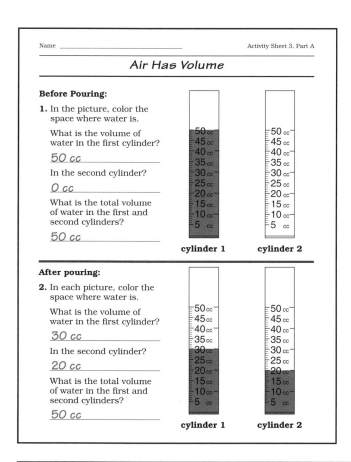

cylinder 1   cylinder 2

After pouring:

2. In each picture, color the space where water is.

   What is the volume of water in the first cylinder?

   _30 cc_

   In the second cylinder?

   _20 cc_

   What is the total volume of water in the first and second cylinders?

   _50 cc_

cylinder 1   cylinder 2

Name _____ Activity Sheet 3, Part B

Air Has Volume

3. Predict: What do you think will happen if you split a volume of air into two parts? Will the volume be conserved?

   Answers may vary

4. With your teammates, construct the setup shown below.

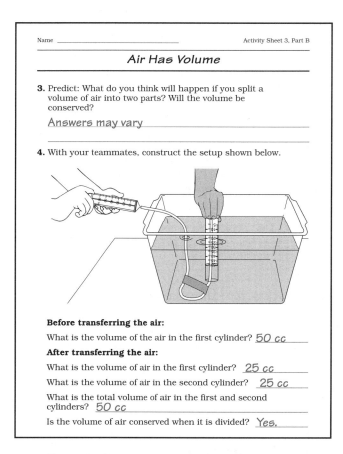

Before transferring the air:

What is the volume of the air in the first cylinder? _50 cc_

After transferring the air:

What is the volume of air in the first cylinder? _25 cc_

What is the volume of air in the second cylinder? _25 cc_

What is the total volume of air in the first and second cylinders? _50 cc_

Is the volume of air conserved when it is divided? _Yes._

Teaching Suggestions

Ask students to remind you of the property of air that they have discovered so far.

Review the idea that air takes up space. Tell students that when something occupies a certain amount of space, we can measure that space. The size of that space is referred to as the substance's *volume*.

Write the word *volume* on the board. Ask, **What other substances that you use every day have volumes that you can measure?**

Tell students that next they will measure and experiment with various volumes of water and air.

Additional Information

1 Air takes up space.

Elicit suggestions of familiar substances and their volumes, such as a gallon of milk, a cup of water, or a box of cereal. List students' suggestions on the board, pointing out the units, such as gallon, quart, cup, or ounce, that indicate a measure of volume.

(Note that although units such as gallons and cups technically describe capacity, they are also commonly used to describe volume quantities.)

Give each student a copy of Activity Sheet 3, Parts A and B. Distribute to each team of four a large container of colored water, two graduated cylinders, and a syringe.

Write *graduated cylinder* on the board. Hold up one of the teams' cylinders and tell students that a graduated cylinder can be used to measure the volume of many different things, including air.

Project the Graduated Cylinder transparency. Ask, **What do you see on the cylinder?**

Write *cubic centimeters* and *cc* on the board. Tell students that the lines and numbers are used to measure cubic centimeters, abbreviated as *cc* and pronounced "see-sees." Tell them that the cubic centimeter is one of the units of volume.

Call their attention again to the projected transparency. Point out that each short line on the cylinder measures 1 cubic centimeter of volume, while the longer lines extending around the cylinder measure groups of 10 cubic centimeters. Use the erasable marker to fill in the diagram from the bottom of the cylinder to the 23-cc line. Ask, **What volume measurement have I marked on the graduated cylinder?**

Continue filling in the diagram to 35 cc and repeat the exercise to confirm students' understanding.

Tell students that they will now measure out a certain amount of water and then split it into two parts to see what happens to its volume.

Have one member on each team dip a graduated cylinder into the container of water and fill it to the 50-cc line. Write *50 cc* on the board and tell students to write that volume on Part A of their activity sheets. Then have a second team member pour water from the first cylinder into the second cylinder until the water in the second cylinder reaches the 20-cc mark.

2 Have teams cover their work areas with newspaper to soak up any spills. Show them where to get extra paper towels if they need them.

Students should observe that it has lines, numbers, and letters on the side.

One cubic centimeter is about the size of a sugar cube.

Students should say 23 cubic centimeters (or 23 cc). Point out that two groups of 10 cc plus 3 cc add up to a total of 23 cc.

3

Point out that it is very important not to spill any of the water.

Ask students to measure the volumes of water in the two cylinders and write down the number of cubic centimeters in each one on Part A of the activity sheet.

Remind them to write cc after each number.

After they have done this, have them add the two numbers together. Then, have them compare the total with the volume of water in the original cylinder. Ask, **Did the total volume change?**

No. If students report numbers that are slightly off, point out that it is difficult to measure exactly.

Explain to students that when something stays the same, it is said to be conserved. Write *conserved* on the board and ask, **Was the volume of water conserved when it was split into two parts?**

Yes, because the total amount stayed the same.

4

Tell students that they will now repeat the experiment with air. Ask students, **What do you think will happen if you split a volume of air into two parts? Will the volume be conserved?**

Have them write their predictions on Part B of their activity sheets.

Distribute one of the fishhook-shaped tubes you prepared to each team. Ask one student from each team to push the tip of the syringe securely into the long end of the tube assembly.

Students may have difficulty pushing the tip of the syringe into the tubing. Offer help as needed. (It should go about 0.5 cm into the tubing.)

Have a second team member place one of the graduated cylinders in the container of water, fill it completely with water, and then turn it upside down and hold it vertically underwater (see Figure 3-2).

Using one team's tubing assembly, demonstrate how to position it to insert and remove air from the cylinder. First, hold up the tube assembly and point out that the plunger must be pulled all the way back in the syringe before placing the short end of the fishhook tube underwater and up into the cylinder.

Encourage each student in the team to take a turn pushing and pulling the plunger of the syringe to insert and remove air from the cylinder. Tell teams that the last student in each team to use the syringe should add or remove air until the water level at the bottom of the air bubble in the cylinder is as

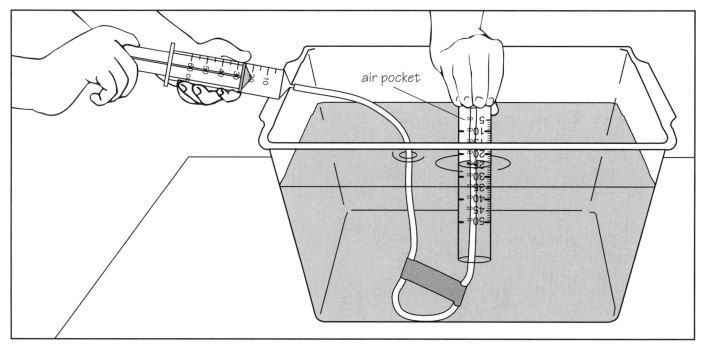

Figure 3-2. Inserting air into the cylinder with the syringe.

close as possible to the 50-cc mark. Have the student holding the cylinder turn it, keeping it under water, so that the rest of the team can see the lines, numbers, and level of the air bubble through the side of the container.

Ask students to count exactly how many cubic centimeters of air are inside the cylinder and write it on Part B of the activity sheet.

Tell the student on each team who is holding the tubing assembly to take it out of the water and carefully push and pull the plunger of the syringe a few times to clear the syringe and the tubing of water. Then have him or her leave the plunger pushed all the way in for the next step in the experiment.

Tell students they will now remove half the air from the cylinder. Have one student on each team insert the tubing into the graduated cylinder again, up to the top of the 50-cc air pocket. Ask those students to slowly pull out the syringe plunger, removing air from the cylinder until the water level is near the 25-cc mark.

Students may have trouble reading the cylinder increments upside down. Help them as needed.

The cylinders holding the 50 cc of air should continue to remain underwater.

The tubing assembly should remain in place in the first cylinder, with the plunger in the same position, until the next cylinder is prepared as described below.

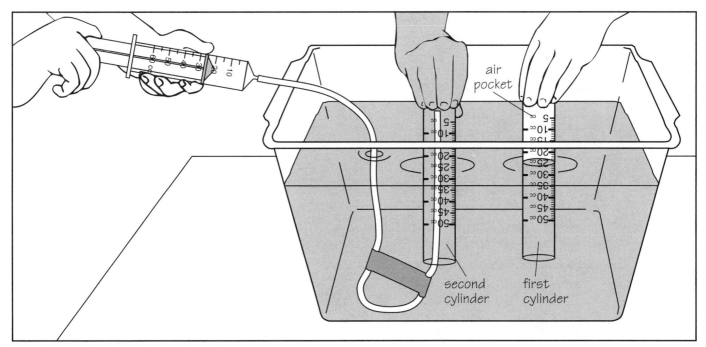

Figure 3-3. *Moving air from one cylinder to another.*

Tell students that they will now measure the volume of air they removed from the cylinder. Ask a third student from each team to fill the second cylinder with water the same way as the first, submerging it upside down in the large container. Have the student still holding the tubing assembly underwater withdraw the tubing from the first cylinder, keeping it underwater, insert it up into the second cylinder, and press the plunger on the syringe.

Ask, **What happened to the water at the top of the second cylinder?**

It was displaced by air.

Have the students holding the cylinders underwater move them around in the container so that their teammates can see the water levels and read the lines and numbers on the two cylinders. Ask students to measure the volume of air in the two cylinders and write down the number of cubic centimeters in each one on Part B of the activity sheet. (Remind them again to write *cc* after each number.)

Cylinders and tubing assemblies may now be removed from the container and emptied of water.

After teams have recorded the volumes, have them add the two numbers together. Finally, have them compare this total with the volume of air in the original cylinder.

Ask, **Did the total volume of air change when it was divided between two cylinders?**

No. If some students report slightly different results, tell them that it is difficult to measure exactly.

Ask, **Is the volume of air is conserved when it is divided?**

Students should say yes.

Have students record their conclusion on Part B of the activity sheet.

Tell students they have discovered another property of air. Call their attention to the Properties of Air chart and write *Volume of air is conserved when divided* on the chart.

Reinforcement

Have students repeat the experiment in dividing a volume of air, this time taking any amount of air they choose from the 50 cc in the first cylinder and putting it into the second cylinder. Tell them to measure and record the volumes for each cylinder. (The volumes should always total 50 cc.)

Cleanup

Remove the syringes and the masking tape from the plastic tubing. Drain and air-dry the tubing, large container, graduated cylinders, and syringes (replacing the protective caps) and return them to the kit. Return the transparency and the roll of masking tape to the kit.

Connections

Science Extension

Give each team a small balloon, a bowl large enough to hold the balloon when it is inflated, and a shallow pan. Have students put the pan under the bowl and fill the bowl to the brim with water. Tell them to push the deflated balloon just under the surface of the water and observe the amount of water that overflows into the pan. Explain that this water shows the volume of the deflated balloon. Next have students fill the bowl to the brim again, blow up the balloon, and submerge it in the water, again noting the amount of water that overflows. Ask students to explain why the overflow is so much greater this time. Students could determine the specific volumes of the deflated and inflated balloon by measuring the overflow water with a graduated cylinder. They also could calculate the volume of the air alone by subtracting the deflated balloon's volume from the inflated balloon's volume. (The deflated balloon's volume will be barely measurable. Help students estimate it.)

Science and Health

Tell students to put their hands on their chests, just above the bottom of the rib cage, and slowly take a deep breath and then release it, and repeat. As they breathe in and out, they will feel their chest expand and contract as its volume increases and decreases. Suggest that students find out more about the breathing process. One good source is *The Air I Breathe* cited in Science and Language Arts, Activity 1.

Students could use the following technique to measure the volume of air their lungs hold in a normal breath: Hold a large, water-filled graduated cylinder upside down in a filled aquarium, put one end of a length of plastic tubing into the cylinder and hold it in place, then take a normal breath and

exhale into the other end of the tubing. The exhaled air will displace water in the cylinder. Tilt your head to read the mark showing the volume of air in the cylinder. Let students compare the volumes of air they exhale while resting, after mild activity, and after vigorous exercise.

Science and Math

The following activities are appropriate for students who are learning multiplication. They should be done in the order indicated.

■ Tell students that the volume of solids is also measured in cubic centimeters. Explain that they can calculate a solid's volume by multiplying its length times its width times its height. Write the formula $L \times W \times H$ on the board. Let students measure various rectangular-solid objects in the classroom (books, a filing cabinet, a storage box), then guide them through the calculations to determine the objects' volumes.

■ An object's or material's volume does not change when its shape changes. To develop this understanding, give each team 20 centimeter cubes, and tell students to arrange all 20 cubes into as many different shapes as they can—a 1×20 tower or row, a 4×5 rectangle 1 cm tall, a 2×5 rectangle 2 cm tall, an L shape, and so on. Emphasize that no matter how the cubes are arranged, their total volume is still 20 cc. Explain that the same is true of air. To demonstrate this, have students repeat the Science Extension above with string tied around the inflated balloon to change its shape.

■ Have students measure the dimensions of the classroom and use a calculator and the formula $L \times W \times H$ to find the volume in cubic meters of the air in the room.

Activity 4
Volume Changes with Temperature

Objectives

Students observe the effects of heating and cooling on a volume of air.

The students

■ observe and record changes in air temperature

■ examine the relationship between air volume and air temperature

■ operationally define *control*

Schedule

About 50 minutes

Vocabulary

control
temperature
thermometer

Materials

For each student
1   Activity Sheet 4, Parts A and B

For each team of four
1   bottle, plastic
1   thermometer, Celsius

For the class
9   balloons, small
1   bottle, plastic
1   *chart, Properties of Air (from Activity 3)
1   *clock or watch, with second hand
8   containers, plastic, 6-L

40   *ice cubes
1   *marker, felt-tip
        *newspaper
        *paper towels
1 pair   *scissors
1   thermometer, Celsius
        *water, tap, cold
        *water, tap, hot

*provided by the teacher

Preparation

1. As advised in Advance Preparation, you will need to have already frozen about 40 ice cubes ahead of time for use in this activity.

2. Make a copy of Activity Sheet 4, Parts A and B, for each student.

3. Stretch the small balloons to make them easier to inflate. With your scissors, cut the neck off of each balloon (see Figure 4-1).

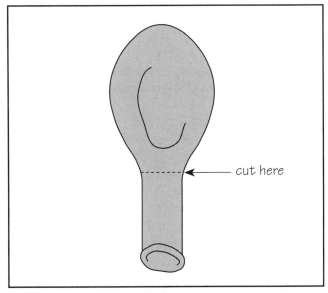

Figure 4-1. Cutting the balloon.

4. For half of the teams, fill plastic containers three-quarters-full with cold water and add at least 10 ice cubes to each.

5. Wait until just before beginning the activity to fill plastic containers three-quarters-full with hot tap water for the other half of the teams.

6. Each team will need a container of water (hot or cold), a plastic bottle, a thermometer, a small balloon (cut), and a paper towel.

Background Information

Everything reacts to heating and cooling. With very few exceptions, adding heat to a material causes the material to expand, and cooling it causes it to contract. We use this principle constantly in everyday life—for example, when loosening a tight jar lid. Even if the lid seems absolutely immobile, it can be made larger and looser by running it under warm water.

The cause of this extraordinary phenomenon takes place at the molecular level. The molecules that make up every substance hold on to each other with varying degrees of strength. When they are excited by added heat, they begin to bounce around, gradually pushing one another further apart, expanding the substance. When they are cooled, the opposite happens: they bounce less and move closer together, causing the substance to shrink.

The molecules in a gas such as air are very loosely arranged; as a result, heating them causes the gas to expand dramatically. This characteristic of air makes the experiment in this activity particularly well-suited for young students, since just the small difference in temperature between ice water and warm tap water will cause such obvious changes in the volume of air that students can easily observe the effects.

When students immerse a bottle in hot water, the water heats the walls of the plastic bottle. The walls transmit the heat to the air molecules inside, causing them to bounce around with greater energy and driving them further apart. The inflation of the balloon on the neck of the bottle is evidence of the air's expansion. Immersing the bottle in cold water, on the other hand, cools the air molecules inside, making them bounce less and move closer together. This time the balloon collapses, evidence that the volume of air is shrinking. The effect is most dramatic when the opening of the balloon just above the neck of the bottle is wide enough so that the balloon is turned inside out and sinks down into the bottle.

Air Volume and Temperature

1. Record the temperatures outside the bottle.

   Air temperature _____

   Water temperature _____

2. After you have placed the balloon over the neck of your bottle, draw the way your balloon looks on the bottle in the picture to the right.

3. Record the temperature inside the bottle every 30 seconds for 3 minutes. Your teacher will call out the times listed below. Write the number of degrees on your thermometer on the line opposite the time.

   Start _____   1:30 _____   3:00 _____
   0:30 _____   2:00 _____
   1:00 _____   2:30 _____

Air Volume and Temperature

4. On the picture of the bottle to the right, draw the way your balloon looks after the bottle has been in the container of water for 3 minutes. Write *hot water* or *cold water* under the bottle, depending on which one your team used.

   What happened to the balloon?
   Answers will vary, depending on the water temperature. Students using hot water should say the balloon filled up with air. Those using cold water should say the balloon collapsed and perhaps even sank into the bottle.

   What is the relationship between temperature and volume?
   The hotter the temperature, the larger the volume; the colder the temperature, the smaller the volume.

Teaching Suggestions

Write the word *temperature* on the board and ask, **What is temperature?**

Ask, **What do we use to measure temperature?**

Write *thermometer* on the board and explain that a thermometer measures temperature by giving a number to things according to how hot or cold they are.

Tell students that, in this activity, they will use a thermometer to see how temperature affects the volume of air.

Give each student a copy of Activity Sheet 4, Parts A and B. Give half the teams the containers of ice water and the other half the containers of hot water. If possible, place teams with hot water next to teams with cold water so all teams will be able to observe the results of both experiments.

Additional Information

1

Students will probably say that temperature describes how hot or cold something is.

Students may say that a thermometer is used to measure temperature.

2

Have teams cover their work areas with newspaper and have extra paper towels handy to soak up any spills.

Distribute to each team of four a small balloon (cut), a thermometer, a paper towel, and a plastic bottle.

Hold up a thermometer and ask, **Which way does the red line in the middle go when it gets hotter? Which way does it go when it gets colder?**

Students should know the red line goes up when it is hotter and down when it is colder.

Remind students to hold the thermometers by the sides. Tell them that if they touch the tube in the middle with their hands, the thermometer will measure the heat of their hands instead of the air.

Ask students to look at their team's thermometer and read the temperature of the air in the classroom by looking at the number closest to the top of the red line. Tell them that temperature is measured in degrees, which are represented by the numbers on the thermometer.

If necessary, review how to read a thermometer.

Poll the teams' results and write the classroom air temperature on the board, followed by °C. Have students record the temperature on Part A of their activity sheets.

Ask teams to place their thermometer in the water in one corner of the plastic container. Count aloud slowly to 15 and then tell students to read and record the temperature of their team's water on their activity sheets.

Next, have them remove the thermometer, dry it off with a paper towel, and wait a minute or two until it reaches room temperature again. Then have them place it inside the plastic bottle.

Ask for a student volunteer to help you prepare a setup with an extra bottle, a thermometer, and a balloon. Call the class's attention to your demonstration. Place the thermometer in the bottle and ask your helper to hold the plastic bottle steady as you stretch a balloon over the neck of the bottle (see Figure 4-2).

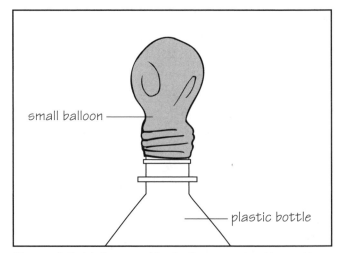

small balloon

plastic bottle

Figure 4-2. Make sure the balloon covers the entire neck of the bottle.

Tell teams to prepare the same setup, with one student holding the bottle and another fitting the balloon over the neck. Check each team's bottle: the balloon should cover the entire threaded neck of the bottle, the opening of the balloon should be centered over the neck of the bottle, and the opening should be wide enough so that air can pass freely between the balloon and the bottle.

Tell students to draw the shape of their team's balloon on the picture of the bottle on Part A of the activity sheet.

Ask, **Is there the same amount of air in each team's bottle?**

Ask, **Can the air escape or enter the bottles?**

Ask, **What is the temperature right now of the air inside your bottles?**

Ask, **What do you think will happen to the temperature of the air in the bottle if you place the bottle in the hot water? in the cold water?**

If students have difficulty fitting the balloon on the bottle neck on the first try, have them simply pull off the balloons and try again. Offer help as needed.

Students should say yes.

No, the balloons keep outside air out and inside air in.

Temperatures should all be about the same as the air temperature in the classroom that you wrote on the board earlier.

Students will probably suggest that the air in the bottle will become hotter in the hot water and colder in the cold water.

4

Tell students they will be observing the temperature inside the bottle for 3 minutes after you tell them to begin. Tell them to write down the temperature on Part A of the activity sheet each time you call out the minutes and seconds listed on the sheet. Say that at the same time they should watch to see what, if anything, happens to the balloon on the bottle.

Have a student from each team hold the bottle by the neck and push it straight down to the bottom of the water in the plastic container and hold it there (see Figure 4-3). Tell teams to begin observing the temperature in their bottle. Begin your timing and call out each interval of 30 seconds, as shown on the activity sheet. At the end of 3 minutes, tell students to write down their final temperature readings. Then ask the hot-water teams, **What happened to the temperature of the air in your bottles? Did anything happen to your balloons?**

You may need to go over with students the abbreviations of minutes and seconds on the activity sheet.

Leave the demonstration setup on the counter or desktop, out of direct sunlight.

The temperature of the air rose higher in the bottles, and the balloons got rounder.

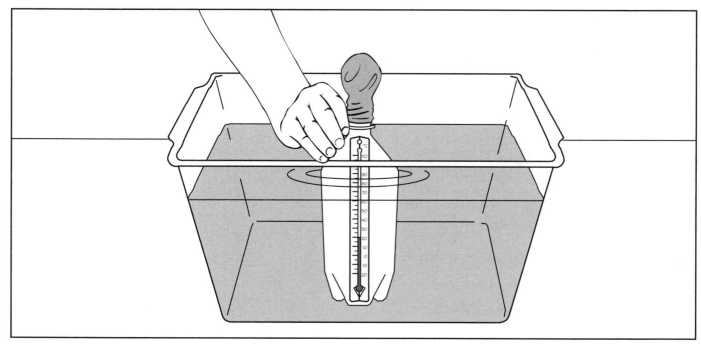

Figure 4-3. The bottle setup in the container of water.

Ask the cold-water teams the same questions: **What happened to the temperature of the air in your bottles? Did anything happen to your balloons?**

The temperature of the air dropped, and the balloons collapsed, even sinking down into the bottles.

Tell students to draw the shape of their balloon on the picture of the bottle on Part B of the activity sheet and answer the question below the picture.

Now point out the demonstration bottle that was left out on the counter. Ask a student volunteer to come up and read the thermometer inside the bottle. Ask the class, **Did the temperature change? Did the shape of the balloon change?**

5

The volunteer should report the temperature to the class.

No. They are the same as before.

Write the word *control* on the board. Explain that a control is the part of the experiment that does not change, so that it can be compared at the end of the experiment with the part that does change. Ask, **What was the only thing that you changed in this experiment—the only thing different from this control setup?**

the temperature of the air in the bottles

Point out to students that if the balloons on the hot and cold bottles of air looked different from the balloon on the control bottle, they can conclude that temperature is what made the difference.

Remind students that they know that air could neither get in nor out of the bottles because they were all sealed with balloons. Ask, **Can you explain what happens to the air in the bottles when you heat it or cool it? Does its volume stay the same? That is, does the air take up more or less space as its temperature changes?**

Lead students to conclude that heating air increases its volume (causes it to take up more space), while cooling it decreases its volume (causes it to take up less space).

Ask, **How can you conclude by what happened to your balloons that heating air makes it take up more space and that cooling air makes it take up less?**

The hot air took up more space by filling up the balloon and making it rounder, while the cold air took up less and less space, finally collapsing the balloon.

Have students complete Part B of their activity sheets.

Tell students they have discovered another property of air. Call their attention to the Properties of Air chart and add, *Heated air expands* and *Cooled air shrinks.*

Reinforcement

Have all the students in the class first stand close together and then spread out around the room. Ask if the number of students changed (no). Then ask if the amount of space that students took up changed (yes). Ask them in which arrangement they would be "hot" students and in which would they be "cold" students.

Cleanup

Leave the balloons on the necks of the bottles as this setup will be used again in the assessment activity. Air-dry the containers and thermometers, and return them to the kit.

Science at Home

Take a balloon, fill it with air and tie it off. Place it on a piece of paper and draw a circle around the outside to record its size. Put the balloon in the freezer or refrigerator for 10 minutes. Then take it out, place it on the same piece of paper, and draw a circle around it again. What is different this time? Let the balloon sit on the paper and watch it for 2 minutes. Trace it again. Did it return to its original size? Why?

Connections

Science Challenge

Make a batch of popcorn for the class. As students observe, ask them what they think causes the corn to pop. Accept all reasonable explanations that relate to expanding air (or steam) inside the kernels. (When the air inside a kernel is heated, it expands and pushes against the hull. The pressure eventually becomes so great that the kernel bursts open.)

Science Extension

Do the following activity as a demonstration. Blow up two balloons to the same size and close each with a paper clip. Attach one balloon to each end of a thin dowel, tie a string to the dowel's center, and suspend it. Adjust the knot's position so the balloons exactly balance each other. Remove the balloons and put one in a warm place and the other in a cold place for about 20 minutes. (The warmed balloon will expand and the cooled one will shrink.) Attach the balloons to the dowel again. Do they still balance? (yes) How can a bigger balloon balance a smaller one? (Both balloons still contain the same amount of air, even through the warm air takes up more space than the cold air.) Remove the clip from the warm balloon and release air slowly until it is the same size as the cold balloon. Do the balloons still balance? (no) How can balloons of the same size weigh different amounts? (A smaller amount of warm air takes up the same space as a larger amount of cold air. The warm balloon now contains less air than the cold balloon.)

Give each team a plastic bottle with a screw cap. Pour a cupful of very hot tap water into each bottle, and have students immediately screw the cap on tightly. Tell students to shake the bottle so the hot water warms the entire inside, then remove the cap, pour out the water, and immediately screw the cap on again. Tell students to watch what happens to the capped bottle. (It crumples.) Ask students to explain this observation. (As the warmed air inside the bottle cools, its volume decreases. The cap keeps air from entering the bottle to replace the "lost" volume of the cooling air, so the bottle crumples inward.)

Science and Health

Along with the other thermometers you provide for Science, Technology, and Society below, obtain one of the newer medical thermometers for taking one's temperature in the ear. Let each student try taking his or her own temperature. (*Caution:* Make sure students clean the probe with alcohol or use a fresh probe cover each time the thermometer is used. Also caution students not to push the probe far into the ear canal.) Let students report the body temperatures they (or you) measured. Explain that scientists consider normal body temperature to be about 97–99°F, although some people typically have a normal temperature slightly lower or higher than that.

Science, Technology, and Society

Provide different types of thermometers for students to examine, such as indoor and outdoor wall thermometers, a candy thermometer, freezer thermometer, meat thermometer, and thermometers used to take people's temperature. Besides ones with glass tubes, include thermometers that have dials with arrows and newer types with digital displays. Discuss the specific use of each type of thermometer, and have students use them in simple investigations. Let students discover that they cannot use some of them because they are designed to measure much higher or lower temperatures than are found in the classroom.

Activity 5
Volume Changes with Pressure

Objectives

Students discover the inverse relationship that exists between the pressure on, and the volume of, a quantity of air.

The students
- measure the volume of air in a container as the pressure on it is increased
- observe the effects of pressure on a volume of air
- graph their results

Schedule

About 40 minutes

Vocabulary

pressure

Materials

For each student
1	Activity Sheet 5

For each team of four
4	*textbooks, hardcover

For the class
1	bag, plastic, reclosable
8	bases, foam, for syringes
1	chart, Pressure Graph
1	*chart, Properties of Air (from Activity 4)
1 stick	clay, modeling
2 sht	dots, blue, adhesive
1	*marker, felt-tip

8	syringes

*provided by the teacher

Preparation

1. Make a copy of Activity Sheet 5 for each student.

2. Before class, collect at least 32 hardcover textbooks of relatively uniform size.

3. To prepare sealed syringes, first remove the caps from the tips of the syringes and remove the plungers. (They will resist slightly and then pop out.) Shape eight small chunks of clay into BB-sized balls and drop one down into the nozzle of each syringe. Replace the plastic cap on the tip. Holding the syringe vertically, replace the plunger and adjust it so that its base rests just above the 60 cc mark. Then, push down sharply, but briefly, on the plunger to force the clay into the nozzle and securely block the opening. (The plunger should stop at about the 60-cc mark.)

   Push the tip of each syringe firmly down into the center of a foam block so that it stands sturdily upright on the foam base (see Figure 5-1). Test each syringe to be sure it is air-tight by placing a heavy textbook on it for a moment. The plunger should move lower in the syringe, but it should rise again to the 60-cc mark when you remove the book. If it does not rise, remove the plunger, press in a bit more clay, and repeat the sealing and testing procedures.

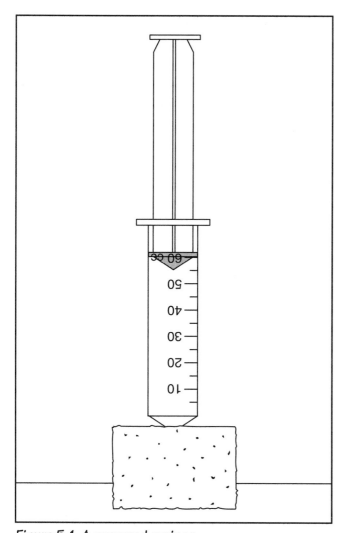

Figure 5-1. A prepared syringe.

4. Post the Pressure Graph chart in a place visible and accessible to students. (Students will need to reach the top of the chart.) Place the sheets of blue adhesive dots near the chart.

5. Each team will need four textbooks and a prepared syringe on a foam base.

Background Information

The previous activity focused on changing the volume of air by changing its temperature. This activity explores another method of changing the volume of air—by adding or removing pressure.

At a steady temperature, air molecules in a container tend to remain at a certain distance from one another. If the molecules are pressed from all sides, they squeeze closer together; the more they are pressed, the closer they pack. As a result, the volume of a quantity of air under increasing pressure continues to shrink. When the pressure is released, the air expands back to its original volume.

In this activity, students apply increasing pressure to a quantity of air in an upright, sealed syringe by stacking books, one after another, on top of the plunger. They observe and measure the decreasing volume of air in the graduated syringe as the heavy books increase the pressure on the plunger, forcing it downward and compressing the air trapped beneath it.

The property of air that enables it to shrink under pressure and expand when pressure is released has many practical uses, especially in vehicles with pneumatic suspension. In place of springs, the shock absorbers in cars use pistons of air, much like the syringes students use in this activity.

Name _____   Activity Sheet 5

Air Volume and Pressure

1. Look at your team's syringe and read the number closest to the bottom of the plunger.

What is the volume of air inside the syringe? _about 60 cc_

2. You will be placing books on top of the plunger one at a time and reading the volume of air in the syringe each time. In the chart below, record what you predict the volume will be when you add another book; then, after you add the book, record the volume in cc that you observe.

Number of Books	Prediction	Result
0		60 cc
1	Answers will vary.	less than above
2		less than above
3		less than above
4		less than above

What is the relationship between pressure and volume?
As pressure increases, volume decreases. Adding more pressure causes volume to decrease even more.

Teaching Suggestions

Begin by asking students, **What did you discover about air as a result of your experiments in Activity 4?**

Tell students that today they will discover another factor that may change the volume of air.

Give each student a copy of Activity Sheet 5. Distribute to each team of four a prepared syringe on its foam base and four textbooks. Caution students not to pull the syringe out of the foam block or to wiggle it around. Point out that the syringe is the same as the one they used in Activity 3.

To refresh their memories, ask students, **What did you learn that *cc* stands for, and what does it measure?**

Tell students that this time you have blocked the inside of the nozzle of the syringe with clay and covered it with a cap so that the opening is completely sealed and whatever is inside the syringe cannot get out. Ask, **What do you think is in the syringe right now, and what is its present volume in cc?**

Have each team place their syringe setup in the middle of their desk or table.

Tell students that they will be using books to add weight to the top of the syringes. Write *pressure* on the board and explain that when something presses on something else it is said to be "adding pressure." The thing being pressed on is said to be "under pressure." Explain that they will do an experiment to find out what happens to the volume of air inside the syringes when it is put under pressure.

Call students' attention to the Pressure Graph chart. Explain that the chart will be used to record the volume of the air in the syringes with different numbers of books resting on top of the plunger.

Additional Information

1 Encourage responses that point out that changes in temperature change the volume of air.

Students should recall that cc stands for cubic centimeter, a unit that measures volume.

Students should be able to say, judging by the position of the plunger, that about 60 cc of air is in each syringe.

2

Ask students, **What do you think will happen to the volume of the air in the syringes when pressure is put on the plunger?**

Student may suggest that the weight of the books will press down the plunger, squeezing the volume of air and making it smaller. Accept all speculations at this point.

Ask one student on each team to read the volume of air inside his or her syringe. Tell students to record that volume on their activity sheets.

Remind them to write *cc* after the numbers in their answers.

Have a volunteer from each team come up to the Pressure Graph chart. Give each an adhesive dot, and show them how to place their dots in the first column at the appropriate level on the chart (see Figure 5-2).

All the dots should be at about the 60-cc level in the first column, labeled *O Books*. Explain that it is okay to place a dot either on top of, next to, or overlapping someone else's.

Figure 5-2. The Pressure Graph chart.

Use one team's syringe setup to demonstrate to the class how to place the center of a textbook flat on top of the plunger, holding the book lightly by the sides to prevent it from falling off.

Remind students not to lean or put any weight on their books as this would add to the pressure on the syringe.

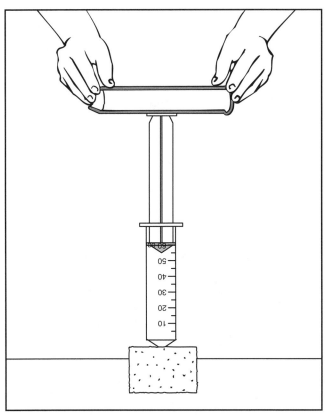

Figure 5-3. Adding pressure to the air in the syringe.

Remove the book and ask all the students to predict what the volume of air will be in numbers of cc after they place one book on the plunger. Have them write their predictions in the *Prediction* column of the chart on the activity sheet.

Remind students to write cc after the predicted volume numbers. Also remind them that it does not mean they are wrong if their predictions do not turn out to be true.

Tell one student from each team to balance one book on the plunger while the other team members observe the syringe. Ask, **What happened?**

The plunger went down in the syringe.

Ask, **Since you know the air cannot escape from the syringe, what do you think happened to it? Why did it happen?**

Students' responses should indicate that they understand that the amount of air in the syringe did not change, but the volume of air—the space it takes up—decreased because the pressure on it increased. They may explain this in terms of the air being "squeezed."

Ask, **What is the volume of air in your syringe now, with one book resting on the plunger?**

Each team should read the number at the base of the plunger and give their answer in numbers of cc.

Tell students to record the reading in the *Result* column of the chart on their activity sheets. Then have one student from each team come up to the Pressure Graph chart and place an adhesive dot in the second column at the appropriate level.

Ask students to predict the volume of the air in the syringe in cc if another book is placed on top of the one on the plunger. Have them write their predictions in the chart on the activity sheet.

Add another book and repeat the procedure until every student in each team has had an opportunity to place a dot on the chart.

Tell students to look at the chart and describe what happened to the volume of air inside the syringe as it was put under greater and greater pressure. Ask, **Can you tell what the relationship between volume and pressure is?**

As the pressure on a volume of air increases, the volume of air decreases.

Have students complete their activity sheets. Tell them they have discovered yet another property of air. Call their attention to the Properties of Air chart and write, *Air under pressure shrinks.*

Reinforcement

Have students lay all four textbooks on the plunger of the syringe setup and then remove them, one at a time, and note each time how much the volume changed. Then ask students what happened to the volume of air when all the books were removed. (The plunger moved back up, and the volume of air returned to its original size.)

Cleanup

Pull the syringes out of the foam blocks, but leave them intact (do not remove the clay in the tips). The syringe setups will be used again in the assessment activity. Replace the caps on the tips of the syringes and return them, along with the foam blocks, to the kit. Place any unused clay in the reclosable plastic bag and return it to the kit as well. Leave the Pressure Graph posted for the remainder of the activities.

Connections

Science Extension

Ask students whether they think water can be squeezed the way air can—that is, whether its volume can be decreased by applying pressure to it. Accept all responses, then have students do the following activity: Give each team an empty plastic soda bottle with a screw cap. Tell students to screw the cap on tightly and then squeeze the bottle as hard as they can. (They should be able to compress the bottle a noticeable amount.) Then have each team fill its bottle to the brim with water, replace the cap tightly, and squeeze again. (Students will be able to compress the bottle only slightly, if at all.) Explain that air can be squeezed (compressed) but liquids such as water cannot.

Science and the Arts

Obtain a copy of *Science Magic with Air* by Chris Oxlade (Barron's, 1994). This children's book presents illustrated instructions for performing ten simple magic tricks that involve manipulating air in some way. Several of the tricks rely on changes in air pressure to achieve a dramatic effect. Encourage interested students to choose one of the tricks and prepare it for the rest of the class. You may want to have students work in cooperative teams of two or three, with one student practicing and performing the trick and making his or her magician's costume, and the other student(s) gathering and preparing the props and critiquing the performer's practice sessions. Let each magician present his or her trick to the rest of the class in a final performance. At the conclusion of each trick, ask the rest of the class to use what they have learned about air to suggest an explanation for the trick.

Science and Language Arts

As a follow-up to Science, Technology, and Society below, explain that when spacecraft reenter the earth's atmosphere, they press against the air with such force that it is heated to thousands of degrees. Provide age-appropriate source materials—a children's encyclopedia, library books, videos, and CD-ROM programs—so interested students can find out more about this phenomenon. Encourage students to prepare an oral report or a bulletin board display describing the materials that are used on the outside of spacecraft to prevent them from burning up on reentry.

Science and Math

Have each team arrange four syringes and bases within 20 cm (8 in.) of one another to form a square shape and repeat the basic activity with the books pressing down on all four syringes at once. Ask students to compare these results with the results they recorded for one syringe. Guide students to notice the pattern. (The weight of the books pressing down is divided among the four syringes. Thus, the decrease in volume of the air in each syringe will be about one fourth the decrease when only one syringe was used.)

Science, Technology, and Society

When pressure is applied to air in a container that does not permit its volume to increase, the air's temperature increases. Students can discover this by using a bicycle pump to inflate a tire, basketball, pool raft, or other rigid object. Have students pump air into the object until it is fairly full and then continue pumping, pressing the plunger as hard as they can. When they hold the pump's tube, they will feel it getting warm as the temperature of the air inside it increases.

Activity 6
Air Has Weight

1 bag   *clay (from Activity 5)
1   *knife, dull
1   *marker, felt-tip
2   paper clips, small

*provided by the teacher

Objectives

Students assemble and use a balance to weigh a quantity of air and discover that air has weight.

The students

■ predict whether air has weight or not

■ use a balance to compare weights of inflated and deflated balloons

■ determine that air has weight

Schedule

About 40 minutes

Vocabulary

balance

Materials

For each student
1   Activity Sheet 6

For each team of four
2   balloons, large (uninflated)
1   base, balance
1   beam, balance
2   paper clips, small
1   pin, balance
4   washers, metal

For the class
8   balloons, large (inflated)
1   *chart, Properties of Air (from Activity 5)

Preparation

1. Make a copy of Activity Sheet 6 for each student.

2. For each team, blow up one large balloon to a diameter of about 20 cm (about 8 in.) and tie the neck of the balloon in a knot. (Balloons less than 8 in. in diameter may not be heavy enough to tip the balance.)

3. Cut eight small pieces from the stick of clay, each about 1 cubic centimeter in size, for teams to use to level their balance beams if necessary. Cut an extra piece for a demonstration.

4. Each team will need the components of a balance (base, beam, and pin), two small paper clips, three balloons (one inflated and two uninflated), four metal washers, and a small piece of clay.

Background Information

This activity introduces students to the idea that air has mass (hence, weight)—the complementary idea to "air takes up space." By observing that air actually does have weight, students will be more apt to accept the idea of air as "something."

An object's mass is a measure of the amount of matter it contains. The molecules that make up air are bits of matter. Although each is very tiny, collectively they can constitute a measurable amount of mass.

Weight is the measure of the force of gravity acting on a certain mass. Although we are really talking about air having mass, we use the term *weight* for the purposes of this activity because the latter term is much more familiar to students.

When a substance is surrounded by something of the same density, it is neutrally buoyant; it will float, and its weight is impossible to detect. (For example, when you are swimming underwater, you cannot reach out and feel the weight of the water above your hand.) Therefore, if we wish to measure the weight of air, we must make its density slightly different from that of the air around it.

By blowing it into a balloon, we compress the air somewhat, making its density measurably greater than the air around it. By comparing the weights of inflated and deflated balloons, students can perceive that air has weight.

Because air around and above us has weight, it presses down on everything beneath it. The effects of air pressure will be discussed in later activities.

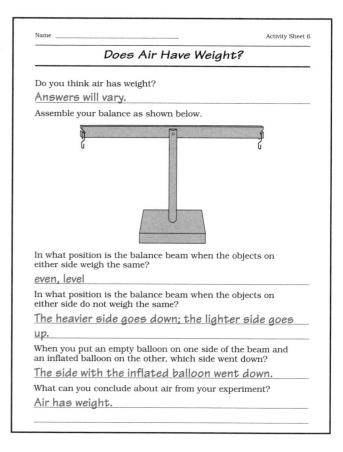

Name _____   Activity Sheet 6

Does Air Have Weight?

Do you think air has weight?
Answers will vary.

Assemble your balance as shown below.

In what position is the balance beam when the objects on either side weigh the same?
even, level

In what position is the balance beam when the objects on either side do not weigh the same?
The heavier side goes down; the lighter side goes up.

When you put an empty balloon on one side of the beam and an inflated balloon on the other, which side went down?
The side with the inflated balloon went down.

What can you conclude about air from your experiment?
Air has weight.

Teaching Suggestions

Tell students that today they will be investigating another property of air. Ask students to name properties of a familiar object, such as a brick, that can be measured.

If they do not mention it, bring up the subject of weight; ask, **Does a brick have weight? Do you think air has weight?**

Distribute a copy of Activity Sheet 6 to each student. Tell students to record their predictions on their activity sheets.

Explain that to find out whether or not air has weight they will need to use a *balance.* Write the word on the board and tell them that a balance is a device that shows which of two things is heavier, or weighs more.

Demonstrate for the class how to assemble a balance (see Figure 6-1).

Point out that the beam should be placed on the base so that notches at either end are on the upper side of the beam. The metal pin should then be inserted through the center post and the beam. Show students where to add a bit of clay to the beam if necessary to level it. Demonstrate how to unbend two small paper clips into S shapes and hang them from the ends of the beam by the larger hook of the paper clip.

When you are finished, disassemble the balance for distribution.

Additional Information

1

Students may suggest properties such as size, shape, weight, and so on.

Students will readily answer that a brick has weight. Answers regarding the weight of air, however, may vary. Students may say that since air takes up space, it might have weight.

2

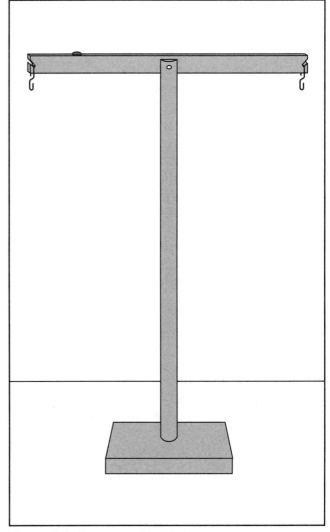

Figure 6-1. The assembled balance.

Distribute to each team of four the parts of a balance—base, beam, and pin—for them to assemble. Also distribute a small piece of clay, two empty large balloons, one full large balloon, two small paper clips, and four metal washers.

Tell teams to assemble their balances. Once teams have their beams correctly positioned on the bases, ask two students on each team to bend down the middle of a paper clip to form an S shape. Have them hang the large ends of the paper-clip hooks from the notches at the ends of the balance beam.

Walk around and check to make sure that all the balances are correctly assembled and that the beams can move freely up and down, coming to rest in a level position. Help students to level any uneven beams with a small piece of clay.

Direct the other two students on each team to hang two washers on each paper clip on their balance beam. Ask, **What happened to the balance? Is the beam still level? Why or why not?**

Students should find that the beam is still level because the washers on both ends weigh the same. If teams' beams are not level, have them correct the balance by repositioning the bit of clay on the high side of the beam.

Lead students to conclude that when the balance beam is level, that means the load on one end weighs the same as the load on the other end. Tell students to describe the position of the balance on the activity sheet.

Ask students, **What do you think will happen if you remove one of the washers from just one side of the balance beam?**

Students may infer that the side of the beam with one washer will go up and the other side will go down.

Have one student on each team remove a washer from one side and ask, **What happened to your balance this time? Why?**

The side with two washers went down and the side with one washer went up because the load on one side is heavier—weighs more—than the load on the other.

Lead students to conclude that when one side of the beam is higher than the other, that means the load on the lower side weighs more than the load on the higher side. Have students describe the present position of the balance beam on their activity sheets.

Have teams remove the washers from the paper clip hooks on the balance.

Tell them to adjust the position of the clay on the beam as needed to level the beam.

Have two students on each team hang one of the empty balloons on each of the paper clips at either end of the balance. Tell them to stick the lower hook of the paper clip through one side of the neck of the balloon just below its lip.

Tell students to make sure the paper clips are hanging straight down so that the weights are equidistant from the center of the beam. When teams have all balanced their empty balloons, ask, **What is the balance telling you about the two balloons?**

Students may find it easier to put the balloons on the hooks if they first remove the paper clips from the balance. It may be helpful to borrow a balloon and a paper clip briefly from one of the teams and show students where to place the hook in the balloon.

The balances should be level, or nearly so, indicating that the two balloons are about the same weight.

7

Ask the teams to replace one of the empty balloons with the full balloon, pushing the paper clip hook carefully through the tied-off end of the balloon, just below the lip, as they did with the empty balloons (see Figure 6-2).

Ask, **What happened to your balance this time?**

The full balloon should have dropped quickly below the level of the empty one, indicating that it is the heavier of the two.

Ask, **What is inside one balloon that is not inside the other?**

air

Ask, **What does this tell you about air?**

Air has weight.

Have students answer the last two questions on their activity sheets.

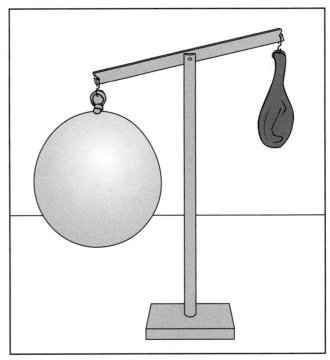

Figure 6-2. Comparing the weight of inflated and uninflated balloons.

Tell students they have discovered another property of air—that it has weight—and write *Air has weight* on the Properties of Air chart.

Review the properties that students have discovered so far and tell students that in the next activity they will learn that thousands of pounds of air are sitting on top of them at all times.

Reinforcement

Give each team two pieces of transparent tape and have them tape an empty balloon to the top of a sheet of paper and a full balloon to the top of another sheet. Have the groups hang each sheet the same distance off the side of the table, and ask them to observe which sheet is bending down more. (The balloon full of air weighs more than the empty balloon and so will pull that sheet down farther.)

Cleanup

Let the air out of the inflated balloons and discard them along with the used paper clips and the bits of clay from the balances. Have students disassemble the balances and return the parts, along with the washers and intact balloons, to the kit. Replace the unused clay in the reclosable plastic bag and return it to the kit along with the box of small paper clips.

Connections

Science Extension

Remind students of the demonstration you did with hot and cold balloons earlier (first Science Extension, Activity 4). Ask them to recall what happened when you made the balloons the same size but one contained warm air and the other cold air. (The balloons did not balance; the warm one tipped up and the cold one tipped down.) What did this show about the weight of warm and cold air? (Warm air is lighter than cold air.) Use either or both of the following activities to show this. Do the first activity as a demonstration; students can do the second activity themselves.

- Sprinkle fine talcum powder on a cloth and shake the cloth lightly above an unlit lamp. The powder will float downward through the air and settle. Then turn the lamp on, wait until the bulb is hot, and shake the cloth above the lamp again. This time, the powder will rise upward, carried by the heated air rising above the bulb.

- Have each student cut a spiral from a sheet of paper and attach a length of thread at its center. Tell students to suspend the spiral above a lighted lamp and watch what happens. (As warm air rises from the lamp, it pushes against the curved surfaces of the spiral and makes it turn.)

Science and Math

Ask students which they think weighs more, their own body or all the air in the classroom. Since we cannot feel the weight of air pressing down on us, students will probably say that their body is heavier. Accept this response without comment. Then remind students that they already know the volume of the air in the classroom (calculated in the third Science and Math activity for Activity 3). Tell students that 1 cubic meter of air weighs 1.2 kilograms. Let students use calculators to find the weight of the air in the classroom (volume of air × 1.2 kg). Then let students weigh themselves on a bathroom scale and record their weight. (*Note:* Do not have students report their weights to the rest of the class, as some students may be sensitive about their body weights.) If the scale does not include metric units, help students convert their weight from pounds to kilograms (1 lb = about 0.5 kg). Have each student compare his or her weight with the weight of the air in the classroom. (Even in a small room, the air generally weighs as much as or more than an adult's body.)

Have each team weigh a deflated beach ball, with all the air squeezed out of it, on an equal-arm balance with paper clips in the other pan. Tell students to count the number of clips needed to balance the deflated ball. Then have students blow up the ball as full as they can and reweigh it. Tell students to figure out the weight of the air alone in units of paper clips (subtract "deflated" weight from "inflated" weight). Have students repeat the activity using washers as the units of weight. Finally, have students weigh the deflated and inflated ball on a sensitive scale and calculate the weight of the air in standard units (grams and/or ounces).

Air Exerts Pressure

Objectives

Students build barometers to monitor changes in air pressure over a week's time.

The students

■ infer that because air has weight, it must exert pressure

■ build a barometer to measure air pressure

■ monitor the changes in air pressure over the course of a week

■ conclude that air pressure is constantly changing

Schedule

Session I – About 45 minutes
Session II – About 10 minutes, 7–10 days later

Vocabulary

air pressure
barometer

Materials

For each student
1	Activity Sheet 7, Parts A and B
1	*textbook

For each team of four
1	balloon, small
1	*bottle, glass, narrow-necked
1 pc	cardboard, corrugated
1	container, plastic, 6-L
1	rubber band
1	rubber stopper, with hole
1 pc	tubing, plastic, thin, 50-cm

For the class
1	chart, Barometer Data
1	*chart, Properties of Air (from Activity 6)
1	Daily Air Pressure
1 btl	food coloring, red
1	*funnel
1	*marker, felt-tip
1	*pitcher
1 pair	*scissors
1	*spoon, stirring
1 roll	tape, duct
1 roll	tape, masking
1 roll	*tape, transparent
	*water, tap

*provided by the teacher

Preparation

Session I

1. You will need to collect one glass bottle (20-oz capacity or more) for each team of four. The bottles must have narrow necks into which the rubber stoppers fit snugly.

2. Make a copy of Activity Sheet 7, Parts A and B, for each student.

3. Make four copies of the Daily Air Pressure sheet. Use scissors or a paper cutter to cut the copies down the middle so that you end up with eight half sheets, a half sheet for each team.

4. Fill a pitcher half-full with tap water and stir in about 20 drops of food coloring. The water should be at room temperature at the start of the activity.

5. Set up a distribution station with the pitcher of colored water, a funnel, a pair of scissors, and duct, masking, and transparent tape.

6. Decide on a place in the classroom where the barometers can remain relatively upright in the 6-L containers, preferably against a wall, for at least a week. They must be kept out of direct sunlight and away from any heating or cooling unit. Students should have easy access to them in order to mark the level of water in the tubing at the same time (and at the same classroom temperature, if possible) every day.

7. Each student will need a textbook. Each team of four will need a glass bottle, a piece of cardboard, a rubber band, a rubber stopper, a piece of tubing, a small balloon, half of a Daily Air Pressure sheet, and access to the distribution station.

Session II
Each student will need his or her copy of Activity Sheet 7, Part B.

Background Information

Air is surprisingly massive. Although we do not normally feel its weight, a cubic meter of air weighs over 2 pounds. The air around us is being pressed down by the weight of all the air above, which extends upward more than 88 kilometers (about 55 miles).

The cumulative effect of the weight of air is tremendous. We do not feel the weight, however, because our bodies push back against the air with as much pressure as the air exerts on them.

A *barometer* is a device that measures atmospheric, or air, pressure. (*Baro* comes from the Greek word *baros,* a unit of weight; *meter* means *measure.*) Traditional barometers consist of a column of mercury in a tube. The column of mercury rises and

falls when the air pressure outside the tube changes. The poisonous nature of mercury, however, obliges us to make a different barometer for this activity.

This second type of barometer relies on a reservoir, or constant amount, of air. This reservoir is joined to the outside air by tubing blocked with a liquid (in this activity, colored water). The pressure of the air inside the reservoir tries to push the water up out of the tubing, while the pressure of the air outside the reservoir tries to push the water back down into the tubing. These pressures equalize, leaving the water balanced somewhere along the length of tubing.

When the air pressure outside the reservoir changes, the liquid in the barometer's tubing moves. When the air pressure outside the barometer increases, it pushes the water in the tubing farther back into the reservoir, and the water level in the tubing falls. When the outside air pressure decreases, the pressure inside the reservoir causes the liquid in the tubing to rise. By marking the initial level of the water, students can easily observe and chart the changes in air pressure from day to day.

Ideally, the temperature in the classroom should be the same at each reading because, as students have learned, changes in temperature as well as pressure would affect the volume of air in this barometer.

Changes in atmospheric pressure are caused primarily by the sun. Energy from the sun warms the air in the earth's atmosphere. As the air molecules heat up, they bounce around more energetically, driving each other farther apart. This dispersal of molecules decreases the air's density, lessens its weight, and lowers its pressure. Higher-pressure air moves toward lower-pressure air. On a large scale, the uneven heating and cooling of air results in the constant movement of air around the globe.

Air Exerts Pressure

1. With your teammates, assemble your barometer. First, study the labeled illustration. Then, follow the instructions below, step by step.

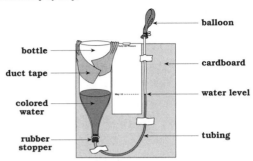

bottle

duct tape

colored water

rubber stopper

balloon

cardboard

water level

tubing

- Insert the stopper with tubing firmly into the bottle of colored water.
- Tape the Daily Air Pressure sheet to the top center of the cardboard.
- Hold up the tubing, turn the bottle upside down, and tape it to the cardboard.
- Loop up the tubing and tape it to the cardboard in three places.
- Tie the balloon onto the free end of the tubing with a rubber band.
- Mark the water level in the tubing on the measuring sheet and add today's date.

Air Exerts Pressure

2. Record your team's barometer data in the chart below. In the first column, write the date each time you check the level of the colored water in the tubing. In the second column, draw an up-arrow (↑) if the water level is above the last dotted line you drew, a down-arrow (↓) if the water level is below the last dotted line, and a horizontal arrow (→) if the water level is even with the last dotted line.

Barometer Data	
Date	Barometer Reading ↑, ↓, or →

What conclusion did you and your teammates reach after recording the water level in your barometer for a number of days?

The air pressure around us is changing all the time.

Teaching Suggestions

Additional Information

Session 1

1

Remind students that the last property of air they discovered was that it has weight. Ask, **Is there air all around and above you? Does that air weigh something?**

Yes.

Ask each student to hold up a textbook. Ask, **Does the book have weight? How can you tell?**

Students should say yes, the books have weight. They can feel them pressing down on their hands as they hold them.

Ask, **If air has weight, does it press down on things below it?**

Students should reason that it must be pressing down, just like anything else that has weight.

Lead students to conclude that because air has weight, it exerts pressure. Write *air pressure* on the board. Explain that since there is so much air above us, the pressure it exerts must be quite large.

Ask, **Can you feel air pressure pushing down on your body?**

No.

Explain that we do not feel the weight of air pressing down on us because our bodies have adjusted to the incredible pressure that surrounds us.

Tell students that today they will build a sensitive device that will measure the pressure of the air around us.

2

Write *barometer* on the board. Explain that a barometer is a device that measures pressure, and the one they will build will measure the pressure of air.

Explain that, by recording the air pressure each day, they will be able to observe how air pressure changes from day to day during the following week or so.

Give each student a copy of Activity Sheet 7, Parts A and B. Distribute to each team of four a glass bottle, a rubber stopper, a piece of tubing, a piece of cardboard, a rubber band, a small balloon, and a copy of the Daily Air Pressure sheet. Show them the distribution station where they will get water and tape.

Give students a few minutes to look over the barometer design and assembly instructions on Part A of the activity sheet. Tell students you will divide the tasks of assembling the barometer among the team members.

3

Designate one student from each team to take charge of the bottle, a second student to handle the stopper and the tubing, a third to prepare the cardboard backing, and the fourth to attach the balloon.

Before the teams begin their tasks, describe the order of the tasks aloud to the class, as follows:

1. The bottle group takes the bottles to the distribution station and uses the funnel to fill each bottle one-quarter-full with colored water.

2. The stopper group pushes one end of the tubing into the wide end of the stopper until it fits snugly and cannot fall out.

3. The board group holds the piece of cardboard in the position shown on the activity sheet and tapes the Daily Air Pressure sheet to the top center with transparent tape. (Tear 2-cm strips of tape for students as they request them.)

4. When the rest of the assembly has been done, the balloon group ties a balloon onto the top end of the tubing with a rubber band.

Suggest to the balloon group that they blow gently into each balloon just to open it up a little (so it will not be completely flat) before they tie it onto the tubing.

Have the bottle group go to the distribution station and fill their bottles with colored water. While they are doing this, instruct the stopper group to fit the tubing tightly into the stopper.

4

Once students have finished filling the bottles, have the students with the stopper/tubing assemblies press the stoppers very firmly into the neck of each bottle (see Figure 7-1). (It is a good idea for you to personally check each bottle to make sure the stoppers are snugly fitted.)

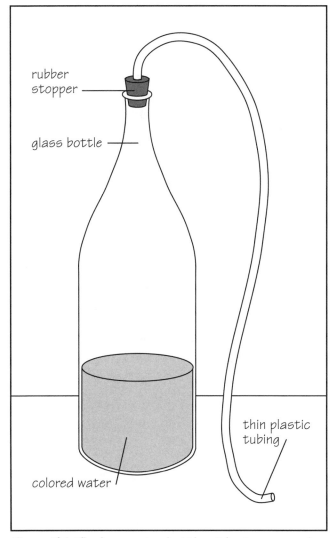

rubber stopper

glass bottle

thin plastic tubing

colored water

Figure 7-1. The barometer bottle with stopper and tubing in place.

Have students take another minute to study the barometer diagram on the activity sheet.

5

Tell each member of the board group to get two 20-cm pieces of duct tape from the distribution station. As the balloon group holds the free end of the tubing above the bottle (be sure to remind them not to tug on the tubing), have the bottle group slowly turn the bottle over and hold it against the left side of the board, next to the measuring sheet.

Have the stopper group hold the board upright as the students in the board group place each piece of duct tape across the front of the bottle and down the back of the board on either side of the bottle (see Figure 7-2).

Make sure the tape is securely holding the bottle in place before allowing the bottle group to let go. Remind the balloon group to continue to hold the tubing above the bottle to prevent the water from running out.

Tell the bottle group students to each get three 4-cm pieces of masking tape from the distribution station. While the balloon group holds the end of the tubing above the bottle, direct the bottle group to bend the tubing in a U curve so that the right side is vertical and the water level is next to the right edge of the Daily Air Pressure sheet. Have them tape the tubing to the board in three places (see Figure 7-2).

At this point, direct each team to place their barometer upright in the plastic 6-L container to help keep it stable while they continue to work on it. Tell them to wedge the base of the cardboard diagonally across the bottom length of the container, from a front corner to a back corner.

Caution students not to tug on the tubing in the stopper as they tape it up alongside the sheet. Tell them the picture on the activity sheet shows them how to position the tubing and where to attach it to the board.

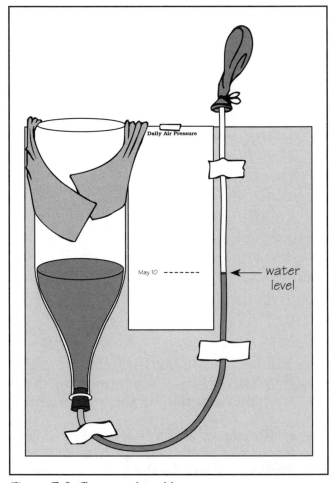

Figure 7-2. The completed barometer.

Have a member of the board group continue to hold the top of the cardboard, however, to make sure the barometer does not tip over as students continue to work on it.

If the boards are firmly wedged into the containers, the barometers should be nearly upright and fairly stable, although they should be gently supported until they are finally placed near a wall so they cannot be knocked over.

Lastly, direct the balloon group to place the balloon over the free end of the tubing and tie it in place with the rubber band. Offer help if necessary. Tell students that the balloon will prevent any water from escaping from the tubing.

Have one student on each team mark the level of the liquid in the tubing by drawing a dashed line at the same level on the Daily Air Pressure sheet. Write today's date to the left of the line.

7 Lead a discussion by asking students questions about how a barometer might be able to indicate changes in air pressure.

Point out the bottle and ask, **What is in the top part of the bottle?**

Students should say that air is in the top of the bottle.

Ask, **Can the air get out of the bottle? Why or why not?**

Students should say no, the water in the bottom keeps it from escaping.

Ask, **If the temperature of the air in the bottle does not change, what else could change the volume of air in the bottle?**

Pressure. Students should recall from their experiment with textbooks resting on a syringe full of air that the volume of air changes as the pressure on it changes.

8 Ask, **If the air pressure in the classroom increases, what can it press on in the barometer, if it cannot press directly on the air in the bottle?**

Answers may vary. Students may suggest it will press on the balloon at the top of the tubing.

Ask, **What do you think would happen to the water level in the tubing if the air pressure outside the tubing increased?**

Students should suggest that the water level in the tubing would move down.

Have one student from each team go up to the team's barometer and first squeeze and then release the balloon as the rest of the students watch the water in the tubing. Ask, **What happened to the water level in the tubing?**

It dropped when the balloon was squeezed and rose again when the balloon was released.

Ask, **What do you think would happen if the outside air pressure decreased?**

Students may infer that the water level would rise in the tubing.

Tell the students at the barometers to grasp the sides of the balloons and gently stretch them apart.

Pressure on the water in the tubing will decrease, and the water level will rise.

9 Tell students they will be observing their barometers at the same time every day for the next week or so. Say that if the air pressure in the classroom rises or falls, they will mark the new level on the Daily Air Pressure sheet with another dashed line and that day's date.

Tell them they will also record their results in the chart on Part B of their activity sheets.

Have two members of each team carry the barometer upright in the container to the classroom location where you have chosen to keep them, out of direct sunlight and away from any heating or cooling unit. It is a good idea, as previously mentioned, to place them up against a wall so they will not be knocked over when teams mark their water levels each day.

Heating or cooling would cause the volume of air in the bottle (and thus the water level in the tubing) to change, as students learned in Activity 4.

10 Post the class Barometer Data chart on the board or on the wall, writing down today's date and the water's height in relation to the dashed line on the measuring sheets.

Today, you should draw a horizontal arrow on the chart to indicate the water is level with the mark. Have students do the same in the chart on Part B of the activity sheet.

At the same time each day, if possible, for the next week to 10 days, have teams examine their barometers, mark the water levels, and record more entries on their activity sheets. Point out that they should compare each day's reading to that of the previous day, not to the original reading.

Update the class chart at the same time with the collective data. Throughout continuing observations of their barometers, students will notice that the air pressure in the classroom does indeed change from day to day.

11 Replace the rolls of masking tape and duct tape and the bag of rubber bands in the kit. Leave the class Barometer Data chart posted and the barometers in place until after Session II.

After students have observed and recorded enough data for them to reach the conclusion that air pressure changes, write *Outside air pressure is always changing* on the Properties of Air chart. Have students complete Part B of the activity sheet.

 Students should have collected data for 7–10 days.

Ask, **What do you think causes the air pressure to change from day to day?**

Answers will vary. Accept all reasonable explanations for now.

If you feel that your students are capable of understanding it, give them the following explanation: The air around the earth is heated by the sun. In some places it is heated more than others. As it warms or cools, its pressure changes. Because higher-pressure air moves toward lower-pressure air, air is constantly moving over the surface of the earth. As a result, the air pressure around us—and everywhere else in the world—is constantly changing.

Reinforcement

Place half the barometers in another spot in the classroom or, if possible, in a sheltered spot outdoors, out of the sun, for a few days. Have students replace the used Daily Air Pressure sheets with fresh copies, mark the new beginning level and the date, and continue to monitor the changes in air pressure. Finally, have them compare the readings of the two groups of barometers and discuss the reasons for any differences. (A temperature differential between the two locations will make a difference in the initial levels of water in the tubing, but if readings are taken at a constant temperature in each group, the direction and degree of the water's movement in both sets of barometers should be the same.)

Cleanup

Disassemble the barometers. Discard the cardboard, pieces of tape, balloons, and data sheets. Remove the pieces of tubing from the stoppers, rinse and air-dry both and replace them, along with the rubber bands, in the kit. Leave the class charts posted until students have completed all the activities.

Connections

Science Extension

Remind students of the demonstration you did pouring water through a funnel into a jar (second Science Extension, Activity 1). Give each student a small bottle of juice with a straw in it, and let him or her sip the juice. Then distribute a lump of clay to each student, and tell students to mold the clay around the jar's opening so no air can get in and out. Then let students try to drink the juice. When they find that they cannot suck juice up the straw, ask them to explain why this happens, using what they have learned about air pressure. (When you suck on a straw, you pull air out and leave an empty space inside it. Outside air pushes on the liquid and forces it up the straw to fill the empty space. With the bottle's neck sealed, outside air cannot press down on the juice to move it up the straw.)

Science and Careers

Tell students that a barometer is one of the most important tools in forecasting the weather. Discuss meteorologists and weather reports that students have seen on television. Invite a professional meteorologist or experienced hobbyist to visit the class and explain what weather forecasting involves. If possible, arrange a class visit to a weather station or the meteorology center of a television station.

Science and Language Arts

Obtain a copy of *What Will the Weather Be?* by Lynda DeWitt (HarperCollins, 1991), an easy-to-read book that explains the causes of weather changes in simple terms and describes how meteorologists prepare forecasts. Read the book aloud to small groups or make it available for students to read on their own. Discuss any unfamiliar weather instruments and concepts to make sure students understand them.

Science, Technology, and Society

Give the following instructions for making a model rocket: Thread a long string through a straw. Have two students hold either end of the string so that it stretches across the length of the room. Blow up a balloon, hold it closed, and tape its side to the straw so that it rides the straw like a sidecar. Release the balloon. Ask students to explain why the balloon shoots forward. (The escaping air pushes against the air behind the balloon, moving it rapidly forward.) Explain that the same thing happens when a real rocket takes off. The burning fuel produces gases that push against the air below the rocket and move it upward.

Ask students whether they have ever heard of or seen a hovercraft. Explain that these vehicles use air pressure to keep themselves lifted just above the ground. Then give teams the following instructions for making a model hovercraft: Punch a small hole in the center of a plastic margarine tub lid and through the center of a cork, and glue the cork to the top of the lid with the holes aligned. (Depending on your students' maturity, you may want to prepare the lid and cork for them.) Attach a balloon over the cork and blow it up through the hole in the bottom of the lid. Pinch the balloon above the cork to hold the air inside it. Put the hovercraft on a smooth, hard surface and release the balloon. The escaping air will lift the hovercraft off the surface and move it along. Students might enjoy using their models in hovercraft races.

Activity 8

High Pressure—Low Pressure

Objectives

Students observe the effects of manipulating air pressure.

The students

■ observe that pushing or pulling on air causes it to push or pull on water in contact with it

■ recall that increased pressure on air decreased its volume and infer that the inverse must also be true

■ conclude that high air pressure pushes and low air pressure pulls

Schedule

About 40 minutes

Materials

For each student

1   Activity Sheet 8

For each team of two

1   cup, plastic, 10-oz
1 pc   tubing, plastic, thick, 20-cm

For the class

16   balloons, large
1   *chart, Properties of Air (from Activity 7)
1 btl   food coloring
1   *marker, felt-tip
           *newspaper
           *paper towels
1 pair   *scissors
1   *spoon, stirring
           *water, tap

*provided by the teacher

Preparation

1. Make a copy of Activity Sheet 8 for each student.

2. Fill each team's cup half-full with tap water. Stir a few drops of red food coloring into each cup.

3. Cut each large balloon straight across, slightly below the widest part of the balloon. Discard the lower (neck) part of the balloon. Pinch the center of the top part and make a cut slightly less than 1 cm (about 0.4 in.) long.

4. Each team will need a cup of colored water, a cut balloon, and a piece of plastic tubing.

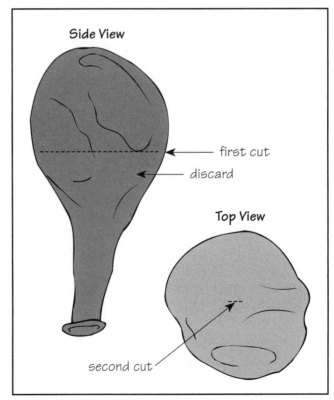

Figure 8-1. Cutting the balloon.

Background Information

In this activity, students create changes in air pressure and observe the effects air pressure can have on another material. The activity teaches two important lessons: in simplified terms, high air pressure pushes, and low air pressure pulls.

Those two principles are evident in objects we use every day. A hair dryer creates high pressure inside that forces air out of the nozzle. A vacuum cleaner creates low pressure (a near-vacuum) inside that pulls outside air and other objects into the unit.

In this activity, the water inside the tubing is, in fact, balanced between two identical pressures—the air pressure outside the cup and the air pressure inside the cup. Each is trying to push the water through the tubing, but the two pressures cancel each other out.

Pressing down on the surface of the balloon that covers the cup decreases the volume of the air inside the cup, thus increasing its pressure. Increasing the air pressure inside the cup, even slightly, pushes the water up the tubing. The amount of water the air displaces depends on how much it is compressed in the cup. The air will continue to push the water up the tubing until it has created enough space inside the cup so that it can expand back to its original volume, at which point the pressures balance out again.

Conversely, pulling up on the balloon increases the volume of the air inside the cup, lowering its pressure. The low air pressure in the cup pulls the water down the tubing into the cup (until the original air volume inside is restored and the pressures are again balanced).

Name _____   Activity Sheet 8
_____
              High Pressure—Low Pressure
_____

Predict:

1. What do you think will happen to the water level in the tubing when you push down on the balloon?
   <u>Answers will vary.</u>

2. Push on the balloon and observe what happens to the water level in the tubing. Draw the water level in the tubing in the appropriate cup below.

Predict:

3. What do you think will happen to the water level in the tubing when you pull up on the balloon?
   <u>Answers will vary.</u>

4. Pull up on the balloon and observe what happens to the water level in the tubing. Draw the water level in the tubing in the appropriate cup below.

What does high air pressure do to other materials?
<u>It pushes on them.</u>

What does low air pressure do to other materials?
<u>It pulls on them.</u>

Teaching Suggestions	Additional Information

1

Tell students that today they will see how air pressure can push or pull on other materials.

Divide the class into teams of two. Have students cover their work areas with newspaper.

Keep paper towels available in case of spills.

Give each student a copy of Activity Sheet 8. Distribute to each team of two a cup of colored water, a cut balloon, and a piece of plastic tubing.

Have one student on each team take the balloon and, holding it by the sides, gently stretch it apart while the other student inserts the tubing through the hole in the middle of the balloon. Tell them that half the tubing should be above and half below the hole.

The balloon rubber should fit snugly around the tubing, making an airtight seal.

Then, while one student steadies the cup on the table and holds the tubing upright, have another student stretch the balloon tightly over the top of the cup and pull the sides of the balloon down over the rim, thus sealing the tubing in the cup of water (see Figure 8-2).

The tubing should extend down almost to the bottom of the cup.

2

Ask students to look inside the cup without touching it. Ask, **Can you see the water inside the tubing? Is it moving up or down, or is it standing still?**

Students should be able to see that the water in the tubing is standing still if it is undisturbed.

Ask students what they think will happen when they push down on the balloon.

Have them write their predictions on the activity sheet.

After they have recorded their predictions, tell students that they will now take turns pressing on the balloon. Caution them to press very gently, especially at first, and watch the tubing carefully.

If students press down a bit too much, water will shoot out of the tubing.

Have one team member at a time gently press down on the balloon, while the other team member watches the tubing in the cup. Ask, **What did you just do to the air inside the cup?**

Students should say they pressed on it through the balloon.

Figure 8-2. Air pressure inside the cup equals air pressure outside the cup.

Ask, **What happened to the water in the tubing when you pressed on the air?**

3 It moved up in the tubing. Some students may have found that a bit too much pressure forced the water up and out of the tubing.

Have students record their results and draw the water level in the tubing in the appropriate picture of the cup on their activity sheets.

Ask, **Why do you think the water moved up in the tubing?**

Answers will vary. Accept all speculations at this point.

Ask, **Did pressing down on the balloon make the volume of the air in the cup bigger or smaller?**

Students should say it made the air's volume smaller.

Remind students of Activity 5, in which they put pressure on the plunger in a syringe full of air. Ask them, **When there was a lot of pressure on the air, did its volume get bigger or smaller?**

Its volume got smaller as the pressure increased.

Point out that when they pushed down on the balloon the volume of the air became smaller. Ask, **When you put pressure on the air in the syringe in Activity 5, what do you think happened to the pressure of the air inside? Did it increase or decrease?**

The pressure of the air must have increased, because when the books were removed, it pushed the plunger of the syringe back up.

Explain that just as squeezing the air in the syringe in Activity 5 decreased its volume and increased its pressure, pressing on the balloon did the same to the air in the cup.

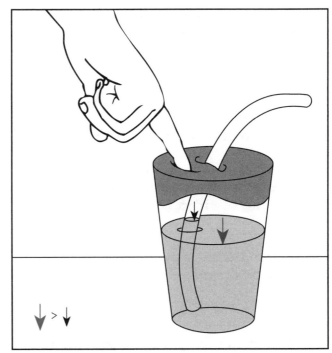

Figure 8-3. Air pressure inside the cup is higher than air pressure outside the cup.

Ask, **If the air pressure increased, should we call it higher pressure or lower pressure?**

4 higher pressure

To reinforce this concept, use your hand to mimic the rise and fall of the water in the tubing. Ask, **Did high air pressure in the cup push the water up the tubing, or pull the water back down the tubing?**

It pushed the water up the tubing.

Tell students they have discovered another property of air. Write *High air pressure pushes things away* on the Properties of Air chart.

Ask students, **What is the opposite of pushing?**

5 pulling

Ask, **What do you think will happen if you pull up on the balloon rather than push down on it?** Have students write their predictions on the activity sheet.

Tell students to gently pinch a small piece of the balloon between their fingers and slowly pull it upward. Have team members take turns pulling up on the balloon and observing the water level in the tubing.

Remind them each time to pull up very gently, so as not to pull the balloon off the cup.

Ask, **What happened to the water in the tubing?**

The water in the tubing dropped. Some students may have inadvertently pulled up on the balloon enough to pull in air from outside through the tubing. They will have seen it bubble up through the water.

Have students record their results on the activity sheet and draw the water level in the tubing on the appropriate picture of the cup.

Ask, **Did pulling up on the balloon make the volume of air in the cup bigger or smaller?**

bigger

Ask, **Then did the air pressure in the cup increase or decrease?**

Students should infer that the pressure decreased. Since they know that a decreased volume increased the air pressure, an increased volume should decrease the air pressure.

Ask, **Was it low air pressure or high air pressure in the cup that pulled the water back down in the tubing?**

Low air pressure in the cup pulled the water back down in the tubing.

Tell students they have discovered yet another property of air. Write *Low pressure pulls things toward it* on the Properties of Air chart.

Have students answer the final two questions on their activity sheets.

Figure 8-4. Air pressure inside the cup is lower than air pressure outside the cup.

Reinforcement

Have students set up the syringes in their foam bases once again but this time press on the plungers with their palms—first gently, then with more force. Encourage them to notice how, as they increase the pressure on the plungers, the pressure of the air pushing back against their palms also increases.

Cleanup

Collect the cups; pull off and discard the balloons after removing the tubing. Drain and air-dry the cups and tubing and return them to the kit.

Science at Home

Encourage students to find tools or appliances at home that use air. Does the device they found create high pressure inside to push air out, or does it create low pressure inside to pull air in? Tell students to ask an adult to supervise them as they turn it on. Encourage them to find out where and how on each device the air pressure is either raised or lowered.

Connections

Science Challenge

The operation of a siphon depends partly on air pressure. Let students investigate this. Have each team fill two clear jars with water. Show students how to hold a length of plastic tubing under water in a bowl to fill it, then hold a finger over each end of the tube and place one end below the water surface in each jar. What happens when the jars are held next to each other? (The water levels are the same.) What happens when they raise and lower one jar? (The water levels change, becoming lower in the upper jar and higher in the lower jar.) Why does this happen? (The water is "trying" to reach the same level in both jars.) What makes the water move up the tube in the upper jar? (air pressure pushing down on the water)

Science Extension

Have teams repeat the basic activity, this time pulling upward on the balloon until the water level drops to the bottom of the tube and bubbles of outside air enter the cup. Then have them let go of the balloon. (Water will squirt out of the top of the tube.) Ask students to explain why this happens. (Air was added inside the cup. When they released the balloon, some water was forced out of the cup to allow room for the additional air.)

Tell students that along tall cliffs, warm lower-pressure air rises upward in breezes called *thermals*. Soaring birds and people in gliders use the "lift" of thermals to stay up in the air for long periods of time. Encourage interested students to find out more about thermals and to report their findings to the rest of the class in oral reports or bulletin board displays.

Science, Technology, and Society

Demonstrate a tank-type vacuum cleaner to the class. Let students take turns holding one hand near the intake tube and the other hand near the outflow vent so they can feel the air being sucked in and blown out. Guide students, as needed, to figure out how the vacuum cleaner works: The motor runs a powerful fan. As air is blown out of one end of the cleaner, outside air rushes in the other end to take its place. Tell them that the pressure of the air just behind the fan is lower than the pressure of the air outside the cleaner. This is why the outside air moves into the cleaner. Remind students of this "from high pressure to low pressure" movement of air when they learn about the causes of wind in Activity 10.

Let students use a bicycle pump again to blow up inflatable objects. As they work, ask them to explain the pump's operation in terms of air pressure. What does pushing on the pump plunger do to the air inside the tube? (squeezes it, or raises its pressure) Why does air blow out of the pump? (Air pressure outside is lower than the air pressure inside the tube, so the higher-pressure air moves out of the pump.) Why does pulling back on the plunger fill the tube with air again? (Pulling back enlarges the space inside the tube, so the air there is at very low pressure. Outside air at higher pressure rushes into the tube.)

Activity 9
Air Resistance

Objectives

Students experiment with parachutes and discover that air resists the movement of objects through it.

The students

- observe the effects of air resistance on falling objects

- infer that the larger the area of an object, the greater the air resistance to its movement

- discover that the faster an object moves, the greater the air resistance to its movement

Schedule

Session I – About 35 minutes
Session II – About 30 minutes

Vocabulary

air resistance
area
parachute
streamlined

Materials

For each student
1	Activity Sheet 9, Parts A and B
2 sht	*paper, plain

For each team of two
2	rubber bands
2	washers, metal

For the class
16	bags, plastic, 30-gallon
1	*chart, Properties of Air (from Activity 8)
1	*marker, felt-tip
1 pair	*scissors
1 roll	string
1 roll	tape, masking

*provided by the teacher

Preparation

Session I

1. Make a copy of Activity Sheet 9, Part A, for each student.

2. The paper that students use at the beginning of this session need not be fresh paper. Used sheets intended for recycling are ideal for this exercise.

3. With scissors, cut each 30-gallon bag in half across the middle before opening up the bag. Discard the top half; keep the lower half, the one with the seam along its bottom edge.

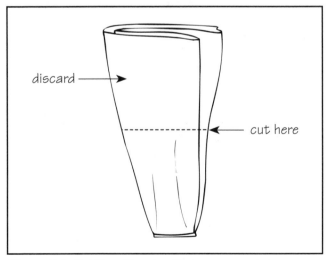

Figure 9-1. Cutting the plastic bag.

discard →

← cut here

4. Cut 64 pieces of string, each 60 cm (about 24 in.) long.

5. Since students will need a large number of pieces of masking tape in the middle of the session, you may find it helpful to tear about 64 pieces, 4 cm (about 1.6 in.) long, off the roll ahead of time and stick them on the edge of a table or desk, ready for students' use.

6. Each student will need two sheets of plain paper. Each team will need the bottom half of a plastic bag, two metal washers, four pieces of string, and access to the tape.

Session II
1. Reserve a large, open space indoors, such as a hallway, gym, or empty cafeteria, in which to conduct the final part of this activity. Outdoors, bad weather or high wind could force you to postpone the activity.

2. Make a copy of Activity Sheet 9, Part B, for each student.

3. Each team will need their parachute from Session I and two rubber bands.

Background Information

As objects move through air, they are constantly pushing the air molecules in front of them aside. Each molecule offers a certain resistance to being pushed aside, thus slowing down the moving object to some degree. This opposing force is known as *air resistance.*

Air is not unique in this behavior. Any substance resists being moved through, the force of the resistance depending on how tightly the molecules of that substance are held together. Air molecules are held together with a relatively weak force and so do not produce a lot of resistance to slow-moving objects. Water molecules are held together more tightly and therefore resist

movement more. In solid substances, the molecules are held together very tightly, making it extremely difficult, for example, to walk through a brick wall.

Bicycling into a stiff wind may provide us with a negative impression of air resistance, but air resistance has its advantages as well. Parachutists depend on it to slow their fall from over 100 miles an hour to less than 20 when they land on the ground. Without air resistance to slow it down, the space shuttle would strike the ground at over 20,000 miles an hour.

The size of the area an object presents to the air as it moves through it significantly affects the amount of air resistance it encounters. In this activity, students discover that the greater the area of an object, the more resistance it meets as it moves through the air. The reason is that it must push aside a greater number of air molecules simultaneously as it moves.

Students also discover one of the more interesting aspects of air resistance— progressive resistance. The faster an object travels through air, the more air slows it down. This is a result of two primary factors: first, for every second that an object travels at higher and higher speed, it must move more air out of the way; second, as that object's speed increases, it pushes harder on each molecule of air to get it out of the way sooner. The combination of these two factors causes the degree of air resistance to climb exponentially with respect to the speed of the moving object. At high speeds, the amount of energy needed to make an object go even faster becomes enormous.

Name _____   Activity Sheet 9, Part A

Air Resistance

1. Follow the directions below to make your parachute.

   • Knot the four strings together at one end.

   • Make a small loop at the other end of each string and stick it onto a piece of tape.

   • Open the bag and tape the strings to its outside edge, spacing the strings evenly.

   • Attach the washer to the knotted end of the strings.

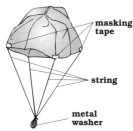

masking tape

string

metal washer

When you and your teammate dropped the plain washer and the washer on the parachute from the same height above the floor and at the same time, what did you observe?

The plain washer hit the floor before the washer on the parachute did.

How does a parachute use air to slow down a falling object attached to it?

A parachute has a large area and meets a lot of air resistance that slows it down as it falls.

Name _____   Activity Sheet 9, Part B

Air Resistance

2. Work together with your teammate to attach the rubber bands to the washer on your parachute. Look at the illustrations and follow the directions below.

   • Hold one of the rubber bands and put the second one halfway through it.

   • Put one loop of the second band through its other loop and pull it taut.

   • Join the washer to one of the rubber bands in the same manner.

When you walked and then ran with your parachute, what happened to the rubber bands?

They stretched more and more as I moved faster.

As an object moves through air faster and faster, does the air offer more or less resistance to the object? (Use the term *air resistance* in your answer.)

Air resistance increases as the speed of an object moving through it increases.

Teaching Suggestions

Additional Information

Session 1

1

Give each student two sheets of plain paper. Tell them to crumple one into a ball and leave the other one flat. Ask, **If you held up both of your sheets of paper at the same distance from the floor and then dropped them at the same time, which one do you think would reach the floor first?**

Predictions may vary. Accept all speculations for now.

Tell students to stand up, hold the papers up in front of them, one in each hand, and drop them both at the same time. Ask, **Which paper dropped faster than the other and hit the floor first?**

The crumpled ball of paper fell faster than the flat sheet.

Ask, **Why did the flat sheet of paper not fall as fast? What did it run into?**

Students should say that it ran into air.

2

Lead students to see that air slowed the paper down. Then explain that this force is called *air resistance* and write the words on the board. Tell students that all substances slow down objects moving through them, some more than others. As an example, ask, **When you wade in deep water or go swimming, can you move as fast as you can walk or run in the air?**

Ask, **Can you think of any examples of air pushing against things and slowing them down as they move through it?**

No. It is harder to move through water than air. Water slows down objects moving through it more than air does, but air, too, resists movement.

Students may mention such things as walking or riding their bikes into the wind, sailing paper airplanes, or hauling in a kite.

3

Write some of their examples of air resistance on the board. Then hold up a crumpled and a flat sheet of paper and ask, **Which of these objects looks larger?**

Students should say that the flat sheet looks larger.

On the board, draw a rough outline of the crumpled ball of paper and a rough outline of the flat sheet, side by side. Write the word *area* on the board. Tell students that area is the size of the outline of an object. Point to your sketches on the board and ask, **Which of these shapes has the larger area?**

Students should indicate the drawing of the flat sheet of paper.

Ask, **Which do you think would be slowed down more by air resistance as it fell through the air, an object with a small area or one with a large area?**

Students may guess that an object with a large area would be slowed down more because it would run into more air.

Explain that objects with larger areas need to push more air out of the way than objects with smaller areas do as they move or fall through the air. As a result, they encounter more air resistance and fall slower.

This is why students' crumpled balls of paper fell more quickly than their flat sheets of paper.

4

Ask students, **What things can you think of that are designed to go fast through the air?**

Students may suggest such things as airplanes, cars, and rockets.

Write some of their examples on the board. Ask, **Do you think these things run into air resistance when they move through the air?**

Students should say yes.

Tell students that, although everything that moves through the air meets air resistance, things that are designed to move fast are shaped very carefully to reduce air resistance. One way of doing this is to make their area small so that they run into less air. Explain that when something is shaped to cut down on air resistance, it is said to be *streamlined*. Write the word on the board.

Challenge the class to see who can get their remaining flat piece of paper to drop the fastest.

Give them a few minutes to shape their sheets of paper. Then have two or more teams at a time come to the front of the class and, at your signal, drop their designs to see which ones hit the floor first.

Discuss the results and compare the different shapes to see what features made some shapes fall faster than others.

5 Tell students they may crumple it up, fold it, roll it into a tube, or do anything they can think of with it to make it drop faster.

The more compact designs will probably fall faster, either those with the weight of the paper pressed into a small space or streamlined with a long, thin shape, such as a rolled-up cone.

Now ask, **Can you think of any situation in which high air resistance would be helpful? When might you want something to move or fall through the air more slowly?**

6 Answers will vary.

Hold a pencil or other object above the floor and ask students to pretend that it is a small person. Ask, **What would happen if this person fell quickly to the floor?**

The person would get hurt.

Ask, **How could air resistance be used to slow down the person's fall?**

If students do not suggest using parachutes, ask them, **If you wanted to fall slowly, would you want the air resistance to be high or low?**

Students should say they would want the air resistance to be high so they would fall slowly.

Ask, **What would meet higher air resistance, something with a small area or a large area?**

Something with a large area would meet higher air resistance and slow a person's fall more.

If they have not already mentioned it, tell students that one design that uses an object with a large area to increase air resistance is a *parachute*. Write the word on the board and tell students that today they will be making and experimenting with parachutes.

Give each student a copy of Activity Sheet 9, Part A. Distribute to each team a cut-down plastic bag, four pieces of string, and two metal washers. Tear off four pieces of tape and give them to each team, or show students where to get the pieces you prepared in advance.

7

Ask students to take a minute to study the picture and directions on Part A of the activity sheet before they start making their parachutes.

Briefly go over the directions with the class and offer help or explanation if necessary.

Tell teams to group the four strings together evenly and tie them together at one end with a simple knot. Have them make a small loop at the other end of each string and stick it onto a piece of tape. Have them fully open up the bags and tape the strings to the outside edge of the plastic bag at every other folded crease, so that the strings are evenly spaced around the bag.

When the teams have finished taping the strings to the bag, direct them to attach the strings to the washer.

Offer help or a demonstration if necessary.

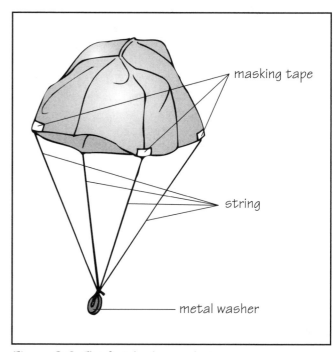

masking tape

string

metal washer

Figure 9-2. The finished parachute.

Have one student at a time from each team test the parachute by standing on a sturdy chair (not a folding chair), holding the chute by the tip of the bag, and letting it fall. At the same time, have the other team member hold out a plain washer next to the washer hanging from the parachute. At your signal, have both students let go of the washer and the parachute. Ask the class, **Which washer hit the floor first? Why?**

The plain washer hit the floor first because air resistance slowed down the parachute to which the other washer was attached.

Let the other teams take turns dropping their parachutes. As teams finish, have them answer the questions at the bottom of the activity sheet.

Call students' attention to the Properties of Air chart. To it, add *Air resists movement* and *Air resistance increases with area.*

Collect teams' parachutes for use in Session II. Return the extra washers to the kit.

| Session II |

Remind students of what they observed in Session I. Ask, **What do objects moving through the air encounter?**

  air resistance

Ask, **Do parachutes increase or decrease the amount of air resistance objects encounter as they fall?**

increase

Distribute a rubber band to each student. Have them take the rubber band with both hands, stretch it apart slightly, and observe its length. Then have them pull slightly harder on the rubber band. Ask, **What happens to the rubber band when you pull it?**

Students should say it gets longer.

Explain that the rubber band stretches when they pull it. The more they pull it, the more it stretches, and the longer it gets.

Tell students that, next, they will attach the rubber bands to their parachutes and look at how far the bands stretch as the parachutes encounter air resistance. This way, they will be able to measure how much air resistance the parachutes are encountering.

Distribute a copy of Activity Sheet 9, Part B, to each student. Have students look at the activity sheet, study the illustrations, and follow the directions for joining their two rubber bands and attaching them to the washer on their parachute.

Briefly go over the directions with the class and offer help or an explanation as necessary.

Ask one student to hold one of the rubber bands while the second student passes the other band halfway through the first. The second student then puts one loop of the band through its other loop and pulls it taut, linking the two rubber bands together. They then attach one of the linked rubber bands to the washer in a similar manner.

Take students to the open area you have selected. Let each team member in turn hold the parachute by putting a finger through the loop at the end of the linked rubber bands.

Encourage them to walk at a normal pace, then walk faster, and finally run, while watching to see what happens to the rubber bands. Coordinate the class so that students are all walking or running at the same time and in the same direction, a few at a time.

As students move faster, their parachutes will run into greater air resistance, pulling back harder and stretching the rubber bands more (see Figure 9-3).

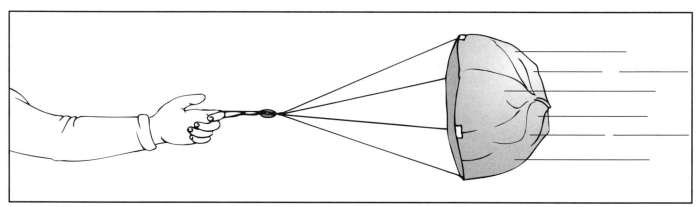

Figure 9-3. Rubber bands stretch to show increasing air resistance.

After all teams have had an opportunity to test the progressively greater air resistance on their parachutes, bring the students back to the classroom to discuss their observations. Ask, **What happened to the rubber bands as you pulled your parachutes faster and faster through the air? Why?**

Students should say the bands stretched out and got longer. Encourage responses that indicate that students understand that the faster they pulled the parachute through the air, the more the air resisted its movement, and the stronger the pull on the rubber bands became, stretching them more.

To sum up, ask, **Does the air resistance acting on an object become greater or smaller as that object moves through the air faster?**

greater

Explain that an object that is speeding up and meeting increasing air resistance can be compared to a person trying to move faster and faster through a crowded room. When something moves through air, it has to push air out of the way, just as you must push people aside when you move through a crowd. It is easy to move through a crowd slowly, nudging one person at a time out of your way, but the faster you try to move, the more people you run into, and the harder it is to get through the crowd.

Call students' attention to the Properties of Air chart and add to it, *Air resistance increases with speed.*

Reinforcement

Provide students with plastic bags of different sizes. Have them cut the bags in half and use the bottom halves to make parachutes similar to the ones they made in the activity, attaching washers as weights. Have students stand on chairs, drop their parachutes, and compare the falling rates of the larger and smaller parachutes.

Cleanup

Cut the washers off of the parachutes. Return the washers, along with the rubber bands, to the kit. Discard the parachutes.

Science at Home

Encourage students to run, skate, or ride a bicycle into the wind on the next windy day. Later, ask each student, **What did it feel like to move against the wind? How fast** **could you go? If you were riding a bicycle and stopped pedaling, how quickly did you stop? What do you think was slowing you down?** (air resistance)

Connections

Science Challenge

Challenge students to see whether they can drop playing cards one by one into a bowl on the floor while they are standing upright on a chair. (*Caution:* To prevent falls, have students do the activity one at a time under your direct supervision.) Let students try different ways to drop the cards, but do not offer any suggestions or corrections. When all students have done the activity, ask whether any of them were able to get almost all of the cards into the bowl. Students may have discovered that dropping the cards edge first does not work. However, if they hold the cards flat (grasp opposite edges from above with thumb and one finger), most will hit the bowl. If students do not discover this on their own, demonstrate it for them. Explain that when a card is dropped edge first, it curves through the air and misses the bowl, but when it is held flat and dropped, air resistance below it makes it fall straight down into the bowl.

Science Extension

Students might like to adapt their parachutes to transform them into hot-air balloons. Look through magazines for pictures of hot-air balloons that students can copy. As needed, help students form tucks in the sides of the plastic bag and tape them in place to make the balloon wider at the top and narrower at the bottom. Suggest that they use a small paper cup as the balloon's basket and place several washers in it. As the source of the hot air produced by a real balloon's gas burner, have students use a hair dryer.

Provide each student with an enlarged version (length about 20 cm, or 8 in.) of the pattern below for making a spinning helicopter. Tell students to fold one blade forward and the other blade back, and to add a paper clip to the end of the long shaft.

When the helicopter is dropped from a height, air resistance under the blades makes the helicopter spin as it falls. Ask students to notice its direction of spin (clockwise or counterclockwise). Then tell them to bend both blades the other way and notice which way the helicopter spins this time. (in the opposite direction) If maple trees grow in your area, point out that their seeds spin when they fall, just as these helicopters do.

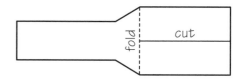

Science and Math

Remind students that they calculated the volume of objects and the classroom earlier (Science and Math, Activity 3), and ask them to recall how they did the calculations. (length times width times height, or $L \times W \times H$) Explain that they can calculate the area of a flat surface by multiplying just two dimensions: length times width, $L \times W$. Let students use this formula to calculate the area of various planar surfaces in the classroom, such as desk and table tops, the floor, a section of the chalkboard, and the covers of books.

Science, Technology, and Society

Show students photographs or a videotape of people parachuting, and encourage them to examine the parachutes closely for construction hints that will help them improve their own parachutes. Point out that real parachutes have one or more holes near the top that let the trapped air escape more smoothly. This stops the parachutes from wobbling and swaying as they fall. Students may want to try cutting holes in their own parachutes to see if that makes them fall more smoothly.

Activity 10
Air Moves

Objectives

Students construct wind speed indicators and use them to measure wind speed at different locations.

The students

- discuss evidence that air moves
- make instruments to measure wind speed
- measure and record wind speed data and discuss possible reasons for differences in wind speed

Schedule

About 50 minutes

Vocabulary

wind
wind speed indicator

Materials

For each student
| 1 | Activity Sheet 10 |
| 1 | *pencil |

For each team of four
1	ball, foam
2	eyes, plastic
1	Wind Speed Indicator card

For the class
| 1 | *chart, Properties of Air (from Activity 9) |
| 1 | *marker, felt-tip |

| 1 pair | *scissors |
| 1 roll | string |

*provided by the teacher

Preparation

1. This activity should be conducted only on a fair and relatively windy day. Check the weather report several days ahead of time and reschedule the activity if necessary. Obtain any needed permission to take students outside onto the school yard. You may also wish to ask parent volunteers or older students to help out with the supervision of student groups around the school yard.

2. Make a copy of Activity Sheet 10 for each student.

3. Cut a 30-cm (about 12-in.) piece of string for each team of four students.

4. Each team will need a Wind Speed Indicator card, two plastic eyes, a piece of string, and a foam ball.

Background Information

Like Activity 3, this activity teaches students how to measure their results in numbers. The wind speed indicators that students make show them that wind speed is another effect of air that can be measured and recorded numerically.

In general, winds near the earth's surface are caused by the uneven heating of air over different geographic areas. The more the air is heated, the lighter it becomes. Warmer, lighter air tends to rise; cooler, heavier air then flows in around and beneath it, creating wind. In addition, the lateral movement of a mass of air at higher pressure toward a mass of air at lower pressure also creates wind.

Students will probably observe two main aspects of wind speed once they are accustomed to using the wind speed indicators. The first is that wind speed is constantly changing. Wind usually moves around irregularly in "pockets" of faster or slower air. These pockets can be seen in the patterns wind makes on the tall grass in large fields.

The second aspect of wind that students will notice is that wind speed is different in different locations. This is due to the effects of eddies or laminar flow. Eddies of air, like eddies of water in a stream, are circular currents that form in front of an obstacle, such as the wall of a building, when air is forced to go around it (see Figure 10-1). Eddies also form on the opposite side of the building as the main air streams turn to reunite with one another.

Laminar flow occurs when air moves over a stationary object, such as the ground. The air next to the ground is slowed considerably by friction as it rubs against grass, water, dirt or pavement (see Figure 10-2). Higher up, however, wind speed increases as the

friction decreases. As a result, any location that rises above its surroundings, whether it is a hilltop, a radio tower, or a jungle gym, will be windier than the area around and below it.

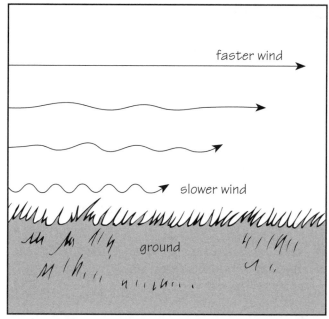

Figure 10-2. Laminar flow slows down wind near the ground.

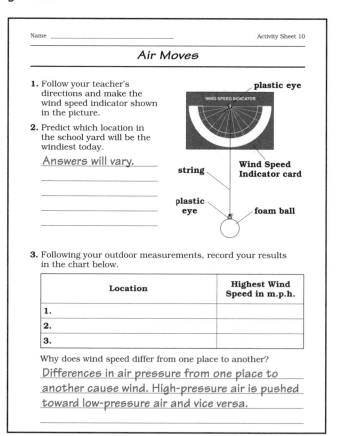

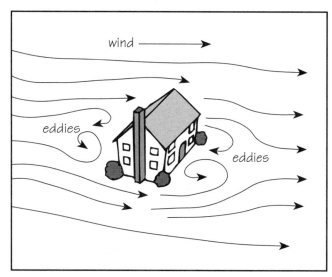

Figure 10-1. Wind eddies around a house.

Teaching Suggestions	Additional Information
Begin the discussion by asking, **Does air move, or is it always standing still?**	**1** Students will probably know that air moves around.
Ask, **What do you call moving air—for example, air moved by a fan?**	Students will probably say "a breeze" or "wind."
Write *wind* on the board and then ask, **Can you actually see air moving?**	No.
Ask, **How can you tell that air is moving if you cannot see it?**	Students may say that they can feel it brush against their skin or that they can see grass, trees, or flags moving in the wind.
Write a list of students' ideas on the board.	
Ask, **Have you noticed that the wind might blow harder on one day than it does on another day?**	Students will probably have noticed this.
Ask, **What does this tell you about the speed of the air at different times?**	Sometimes the air moves faster than it does at other times. Its speed varies.
Tell students that today they will make a device to measure how fast the air is moving. Write *wind speed indicator* on the board.	**2** Explain that a wind speed indicator indicates, or tells, the speed of the wind.
Give each student a copy of Activity Sheet 10. Distribute to each team of four a Wind Speed Indicator card, a piece of string, two plastic eyes, and a foam ball.	
Tell students to look at the picture on the activity sheet and follow the directions for assembling their wind speed indicators.	Briefly go over the directions with students.
Have teams first push the arrow tip on one of the plastic eyes straight down into the foam ball and the arrow tip on the other eye through the hole near the top of the Wind Speed Indicator card. Then tell them to tie one end of the string to each plastic eye, so that the foam ball can swing freely back and forth below the card (see Figure 10-3).	
Borrow one team's setup and point out the two different numbered scales on the Wind Speed Indicator card. Tell students they	

represent two different scales for measuring wind speed.

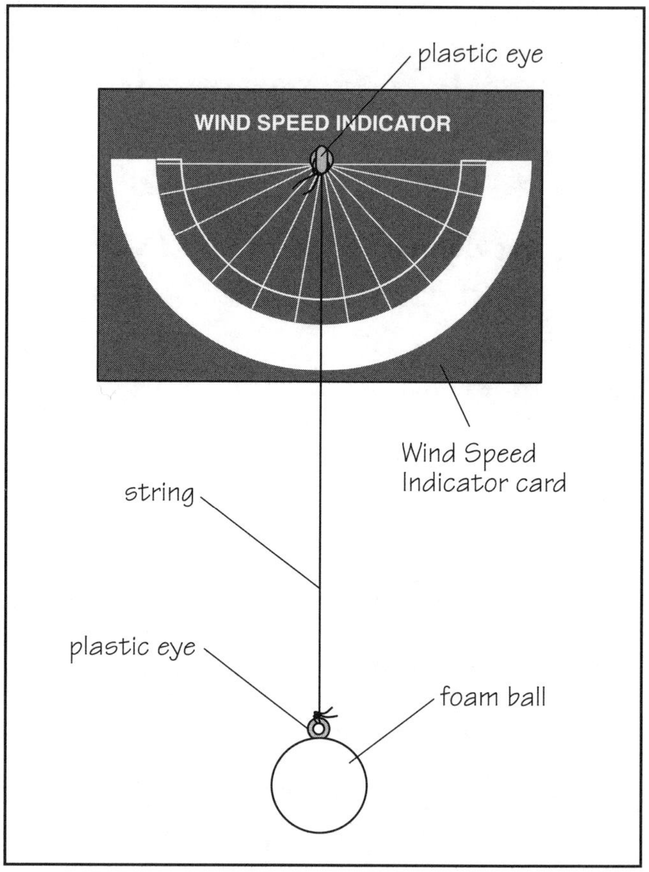

Figure 10-3. The finished wind speed indicator.

The lower scale, called the *Beaufort Scale*, measures wind on a scale of 0 to 12 by describing its effects on land and on water as its force increases.

Wind at force 0 is calm; wind at force 12 is a hurricane.

Tell students the scale they will use in this activity to read and record wind speed, however, is the scale above it on the card—the one that measures wind speed in miles per hour.

Point out that we use the same m.p.h. scale to measure the speed of a car driving along a road.

Ask students in which area, or areas, of the school yard they think the wind will blow the strongest today.

3 Have them write their predictions on the activity sheet.

Poll the teams and list on the board, under the heading *Location,* the various locations on the school grounds where they want to measure the wind speed. Number the locations as you list them.

If you do not approve of a suggested location, ask the team to choose another. It is a good idea to make a copy of the list for yourself and take it with you when you conduct the outdoor activity.

Have each team choose three locations from the list where they will measure wind speed. Tell them to write these locations in the chart on their activity sheets.

Tell students that they will use their wind speed indicators to find out how many miles per hour the wind is blowing in these three locations. Ask each team to take their wind speed indicator, activity sheets, and pencils and follow you outside to the school yard.

Once outside, demonstrate to students how to use the wind speed indicator.

4 Grasp the top of the card and hold it vertically as you turn it slowly from side to side until you have found the direction that blows the foam ball and string to the highest point on the card.

Ask, **Is the wind speed constant, or does it change?**

The wind speed is constantly changing. One moment it may be strong and gusty; the next moment it may be gentle and light.

Point out that today they are trying to find the strongest wind in the school yard and so should record the strength of the strongest gusts they find.

Tell students that as they move around they should try to find and record the highest reading at each location.

Advise students to spread out as they work.

Tell them that if they group together they could block the wind from reaching their indicators.

Have each team read and record the wind speed at the starting location before they spread out and test the wind speed at the locations they specified on their activity sheets.

Assign a parent volunteer or older student to each group and have them accompany the younger students to their various locations. Alternatively, depending on the level of your class, you could have them move around together as a group from one location to the next.

Offer any advice and assistance students may need as they check the sites on their list and record the information on their activity sheets.

After teams have completed their observations, call them together and lead them back to the classroom.

5 Back in the classroom, draw a column beside the numbered list of locations on the board. Write *Highest Wind Speed in m.p.h.* above the column. Have students compare their data by pointing to each location in the list on the board and asking each team in turn, **What is the highest wind speed you recorded at this location?**

Answers will vary.

Write only one number in each column opposite each location—the highest wind speed recorded by any team at that location.

Ask, **Can you tell from the numbers on the board which locations were windier than others? Which ones were they? Which were the least windy?**

Students should be able to tell from the numbers which locations had the most and the least wind.

Ask, **Why do you think the wind was strongest in those locations?**

Answers will vary. Accept all speculations for now.

Explain that in some places the air pressure is higher and in other places it is lower. Ask, **Who can review the Properties of Air chart and tell me what high-pressure air does to the things around it?**

High-pressure air pushes things away.

Tell students that one of the things it pushes away is the air around it.

Then ask, **What does low-pressure air do?**

Low-pressure air pulls things toward it.

Tell students that air at low pressure will pull air in toward it.

Illustrate this point by drawing a diagram on the board (see Figure 10-4). Draw a large, roughly circular shape, and in the center label it *High Pressure*. Draw arrows pointing away from the outside of the shape in all directions.

A few centimeters below this shape, draw another large, roughly circular shape, write *Low Pressure* in the center, and draw arrows from the inside edge of the shape pointing inward toward the label in the center.

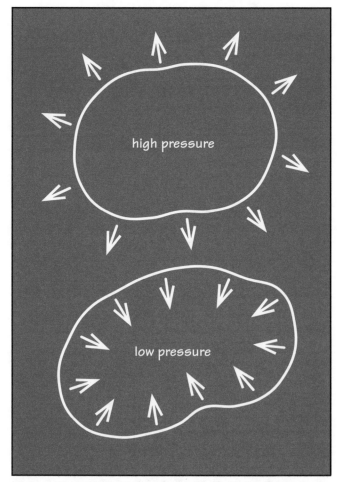

Figure 10-4. High air pressure pushes. Low air pressure pulls.

Ask, **If high-pressure areas push air away from them and low-pressure areas pull air toward them, how do you think this affects the air?**

Students should realize that this pushing and pulling of air creates wind.

Ask, **What did your barometers show you in Activity 7?**

Students should recall that air pressure changed from day to day. They may have observed that it even changed from hour to hour, if they had observed their barometers more frequently.

Tell students that air pressure all around us is constantly changing, pushing and pulling air around, and creating wind.

Call students' attention to the Properties of Air chart. To it, add *High pressure and low pressure air cause wind.*

Have students answer the final question on the activity sheet.

Reinforcement

Have one student blow on the foam ball hanging from the wind speed indicator while another student measures the speed of the airstream. How fast a wind can students blow? Estimate the average wind speed of the breath that students blow and write it on the board.

Cleanup

Cut off and discard the string from both plastic eyes on the wind speed indicators. Remove the eyes from the foam balls, but leave them in the cards. Return the cards, foam balls, plastic eyes, and remaining roll of string to the kit.

Science at Home

Suggest that students, on the next windy day, walk out onto a lawn or other grassy area. Tell them to pick a few blades of grass, hold them up as high as possible, and let them go. Have them notice which way they go and how far they travel before they drop to the ground. Tell students then to wait until the wind dies down and repeat the test. Have them notice whether the grass falls closer to them or farther away. Tell students that this is the simplest form of wind speed indicator.

Connections

Science Challenge

The Beaufort scale—developed in the early 1800s by British admiral Francis Beaufort—ranks winds from force 0 (calm) to force 12 (hurricane) according to their visible effects on objects. Ask volunteers to find examples of the Beaufort scale in science activity books and textbooks. Choose a scale that includes drawings of visible effects, and make photocopies for the class. Let students make observations each day and use the scale to determine the wind force.

Science Extension

Tell students that a wind's direction can be changed by mountains and other large objects in its path. Use the following activity to demonstrate this effect: Build a "mountain" by stacking books in a pile roughly the shape of a pyramid with a flattened top. Position an electric fan about 1 m (1 yd) from the "mountain" so it blows a strong breeze at it. Hold one end of a long strip of tissue paper in front of the fan and let it stream over the "mountain." Students will see that it moves upward on the fan side of the "mountain" and then suddenly downward on the opposite side. Explain that these winds, called *updrafts* and *downdrafts*, can be very strong. In mountainous areas, airplane pilots must be careful to avoid these winds.

Science and the Arts

Find (or ask students to find) instructions in science activity books for making different types of kites, and let students design and build their own kites. Provide a wide variety of construction materials so students can decorate their kites to create animals, faces, or any other design they wish. Let students test their kites on windy days and make any adjustments needed for the kites to fly successfully. (Make sure the kite-flying area is not close to telephone wires, trees, or buildings.) You may want to plan a school kite festival so students can show and demonstrate their creations to other classes.

If you do not have access to a kite-flying area outdoors, you could instead have students make wind chimes. Hang a simple wind chime in the classroom so students can see how it is made. Suggest that they make their own by suspending small objects from a wire coat hanger. Provide a variety of objects for students to choose from, such as metal items from a hardware store, shells, and pieces of broken pottery flowerpots.

Science and Social Studies

As a follow-up to the first Science and the Arts activity above, students might enjoy reading about kite festivals held in Japan and in some United States cities. If a nearby community holds a kite festival during the school year, try to arrange a field trip so students can observe it and perhaps participate with the kites they made.

Science, Technology, and Society

Windmills of various types have been used for thousands of years to convert the energy of moving air to mechanical energy for grinding grain and pumping water. Today, windmills of "high-tech" design are used to convert the wind's energy to electrical energy. Show students pictures of windmills, then have them make the following model, a pinwheel: Cut a 20-cm (8-in.) square from stiff paper, and draw lines to connect the opposite corners. Cut along each line about 10 cm (4 in.) from the corner, to make four blades. Curl one corner of each blade into the center, and push a pin through the center and into the eraser on a pencil. The blades will turn when the pinwheel is held up in a breeze, swung through the air, or blown on.

The Bernoulli Effect

Objectives

Students discover what happens to the air pressure in a stream of air as it moves rapidly through a narrow space.

The students
- construct a device that indicates a pressure drop in a fast-moving stream of air

- observe that two foam balls move toward one another as air flows between them

- operationally define the *Bernoulli effect*

Schedule

About 40 minutes

Vocabulary

Bernoulli effect

Materials

For each student
1   Activity Sheet 11

For each team of four
1   trapezoid piece

For the class
16   balls, foam
1   *chart, Properties of Air (from Activity 10)
1   *marker, felt-tip
16   paper clips, large
1 roll   tape, masking

*provided by the teacher

Preparation

1. Make a copy of Activity Sheet 11 for each student.

2. Bend open the large paper clips and straighten each one out except for the smaller hook in one end. Insert the straightened long end into the hole in each foam ball and push it all the way through the ball until the small hook is buried in the ball. Bend the tip of the long end to the side to form a right angle (see Figure 11-2).

3. Each group of four students will need two foam balls (with paper clips inserted), a trapezoid piece, and four 4-cm (about 1.6-in.) pieces of masking tape.

Background Information

Air pressure in a certain space depends to a large degree on the density of air molecules in that space. The more molecules, the higher the air pressure. Conversely, the fewer molecules, the lower the air pressure.

An interesting phenomenon occurs when moving air is squeezed through a narrow opening: the molecules of air behave much like cars moving in heavy traffic on a four-lane highway when they are all suddenly forced to merge into one lane. The molecules bunch up in front of the narrow passage, raising the density and pressure of the air at that point. As the molecules pass through the narrow opening, they speed up and spread out, becoming less densely packed. The result is a decrease in air

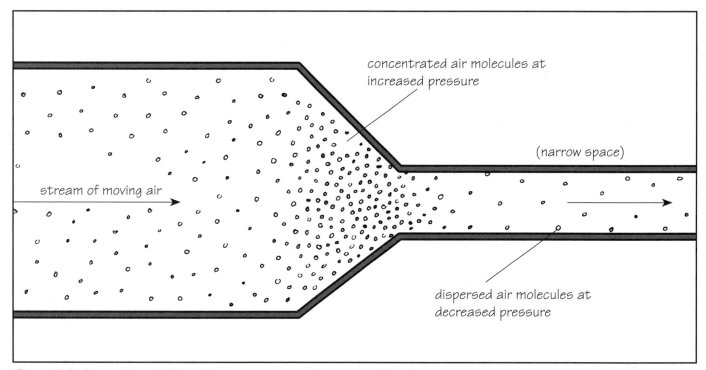

concentrated air molecules at increased pressure

(narrow space)

stream of moving air

dispersed air molecules at decreased pressure

Figure 11-1. Squeezing air through a narrow space decreases its pressure.

pressure in that narrow space (although the air soon returns to normal density and pressure on the other side). The narrower the space the air is squeezed through, the lower its pressure drops (see Figure 11-1).

This phenomenon was noted and studied by a Swiss scientist named Daniel Bernoulli, who came from a prominent family of mathematicians, and it is now known as the *Bernoulli effect*. It has many practical applications, most notably in the design of an airplane's wing. Air moves faster over a wing's curved upper surface than over the flatter lower surface, thus lowering its relative pressure and providing the "lift" that enables the airplane to fly.

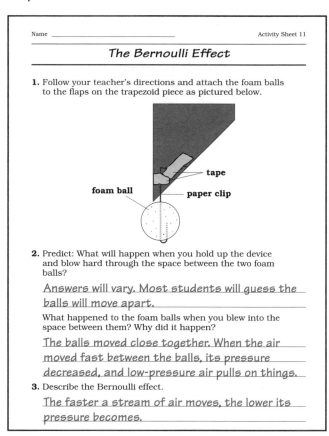

Name _____ Activity Sheet 11

The Bernoulli Effect

1. Follow your teacher's directions and attach the foam balls to the flaps on the trapezoid piece as pictured below.

tape

foam ball   paper clip

2. Predict: What will happen when you hold up the device and blow hard through the space between the two foam balls?

   Answers will vary. Most students will guess the balls will move apart.

   What happened to the foam balls when you blew into the space between them? Why did it happen?

   The balls moved close together. When the air moved fast between the balls, its pressure decreased, and low-pressure air pulls on things.

3. Describe the Bernoulli effect.

   The faster a stream of air moves, the lower its pressure becomes.

Teaching Suggestions

Tell students that today they will make a device that demonstrates what happens to the pressure of moving air when it is forced to pass through a narrow space.

Give each student a copy of Activity Sheet 11. Distribute to each team of four a trapezoid piece and two foam balls prepared with paper clips.

Borrow a trapezoid piece, a foam ball, and two pieces of masking tape from one of the teams and demonstrate to the class how to attach the paper clip to the end of one triangular flap on the trapezoid piece so that the foam ball hangs just below the bottom corner.

Have teams finish constructing the devices.

Instruct one member of each team to hold up the device by its rectangular base and show the rest of the team how the flaps of the trapezoid piece hang down and can swing freely back and forth. Then have them set their devices aside for a few minutes.

Additional Information

Have one member of each team bend down the sides of the trapezoid piece along the scores, creasing the folds and then moving the flaps back and forth until they dangle freely.

The paper clips should be attached to the outside of the flaps (see Figure 11-3).

Walk around and check to see that the flaps can move freely and that the paper clips are securely taped to each flap.

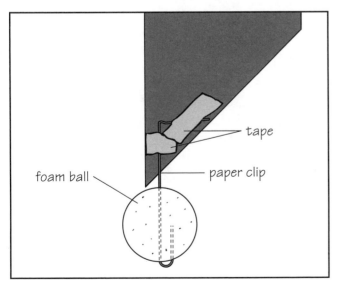

Figure 11-2. Attaching the foam ball to the flap of the trapezoid piece.

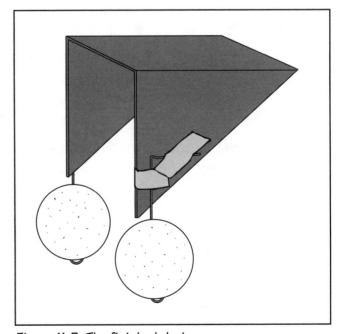

Figure 11-3. The finished device.

Ask, **What do you think will happen if you blow between the foam balls?**

 2 Answers may vary, but most students will probably guess that the balls will move apart.

Have students write their predictions on the activity sheet.

Ask one member of each team to hold up the device again and blow through the space between the foam balls. Tell the student to blow gently at first and then harder, while the rest of the team observes the result. Ask, **What happened to the foam balls?**

Most students will be surprised that the balls moved closer together.

Allow each student on the teams to take a turn, encouraging the other team members to watch to see if the same thing happens when everyone else blows. Have students record the results of their experiment on their activity sheets.

Ask, **What do you think could have caused the foam balls to move together?**

3 Accept all speculations at this point.

If students have not suggested it, explain that the "secret force" that brought the balls together has something to do with air pressure.

Call students' attention to the Properties of Air chart. Ask, **What kind of air pressure pulls on things—high pressure or low pressure?**

Students should say that low pressure pulls, high pressure pushes.

Ask, **When you blew air between the balls, and the balls moved closer together, do you think the air pressure between them became higher or lower?**

Since the balls were pulled together, the air pressure between them must have become lower.

Ask, **As you blew harder, what happened to the balls? Why?**

Students should say that the foam balls came even closer together when they blew harder. They may be able to reason that the harder they blew, the more the air pressure between the balls decreased.

Point out to students that as they blew harder, the speed of the air moving between the balls increased.

Write *Bernoulli effect* on the board. Explain that Bernoulli was a Swiss scientist who noticed the effect they have just

4

demonstrated and realized that the pressure in a stream of air moving through a narrow space decreases as its speed increases.

On the Properties of Air chart, write, *The faster a stream of air moves through a narrow space, the lower its pressure.*

If students understand that air is composed of molecules, you could explain to them that when air molecules are forced through a narrow opening they have to go faster to all fit through. As they move faster, they spread apart. The fewer air molecules there are in a given space, the lower the air pressure is in that space. Thus, the pressure drops in a stream of moving air. If a diagram would be helpful, draw Figure 11-1 on the board.

Tell students to complete their activity sheets.

Reinforcement

Have students hang other lightweight objects on the trapezoid piece in place of the foam balls and repeat the experiment, first blowing very softly, then harder, and then very hard. Ask them to notice how much the distance between the objects varies, depending on how hard they blow.

Cleanup

Remove and discard the tape from the trapezoid pieces and the paper clips from the foam balls. Replace the trapezoid pieces, foam balls, box of large paper clips, and roll of masking tape in the kit.

Connections

Science Challenge

Reverse the hose connection on a tank-type vacuum cleaner so it blows air out instead of sucking it in. Ask students what they think will happen if you blow air upward with the vacuum cleaner and then put a table tennis ball above the hose. (Students will undoubtedly think that the air will blow the ball away.) Place the ball near the end of the hose and let go. It will hover in mid-air above the hose. If you tilt the hose, the ball will still stay in the airstream. Explain (or ask students to try to explain) the cause of this effect. (The faster-moving, low-pressure air around the ball pulls it into the center of the airstream and holds it there.)

Science Extension

The Bernoulli effect—simply a difference in air pressure—provides the lift needed to raise an airplane into the air and keep it up despite its tremendous weight. Let the class investigate lift in the following activities, which should be done in the order given.

Observing lift. Have each student tuck one end of a narrow paper strip into a book and hold the book horizontally. What happens to the strip. (It droops down.) Now tell students to hold the book just below their chin, with the strip facing away from them, and blow air over the top. What happens? (The strip lifts up and stays parallel with the book for as long as they blow.) Guide students to recall what happened when they blew between the two foam balls and what they learned about moving air in this activity (faster-moving air has lower pressure than slower-moving air) and in Activity 8 (high air pressure pushes things, low air pressure pulls things). Then ask them to explain the lifting of the paper strip in terms of air pressure. (Blowing across the top of the strip made the air pressure lower above it. The lower pressure above pulled

the strip up, while the higher pressure below pushed it up.) Tell students that the same thing happens with airplane wings when a plane rushes down the runway to take off. The pull of lower air pressure above the wing is called *lift*.

Modeling a wing. Give each team the following instructions for making a simple model of an airplane wing: From a sheet of stiff paper, cut a strip about 4 cm wide and 25 cm long (1.6 in. × 10 in.). Draw a line across the strip about 12 cm (4.8 in.) from one short edge. Fold the strip along the line and crease it sharply, then align the two short edges and tape them together. (The unequal lengths of the two sections will make the top section curve, forming a wing shape.) Use a pencil to poke a small hole through the top and bottom of the wing, midway between the sides and a bit closer to the front (the fold) than the back. Cut a drinking straw in half and push it through the holes, then thread a long string through the straw. Finally, hold the string vertically (with the curved part of the wing on top), pull it taut, and blow at the front of the wing. The moving air will provide lift, and the wing will rise up the thread. (You may want to provide a fan or hair dryer so students can maintain a steady flow of air on the wing.)

Science, Technology, and Society

Encourage interested students to find and examine pictures of airplanes that clearly show the curved upper surface of the wings. Provide a variety of source materials, including videos and CD-ROMs. Point out that although helicopters do not have wings, they still depend on lift to fly; the helicopter blades provide the lift.

Activity 12
Paper Airplanes

Objectives

Students experiment with paper airplanes to determine what makes an airplane fly well.

The students
- make and test two glider designs for performance
- discuss the variables that affect a glider's flight
- modify their glider designs to try to improve their performance

Schedule

Session I – About 50 minutes
Session II – About 50 minutes

Vocabulary

dart
glider
slider
variable

Materials

For each student
1	Activity Sheet 12, Parts A and B
1 sht	*paper, plain
1	*pencil

For each team of four
1	measuring tape

For the class
1	Dart Design
1 box	paper clips, small
1	Slider Design
1	*stopwatch, or watch with second hand
1 roll	tape, masking

*provided by the teacher

Preparation

Session I
1. Today's activity again calls for a large, open space—in this case for flying paper airplanes. Results will be most consistent in still air, so try to reserve an indoor space, such as the gym; if one is not available, take students outside, weather permitting, for the flights. As a last resort, slide the desks or tables to one side of the classroom and use the other side for flying.

2. Make a copy of Activity Sheet 12, Part A, for each student.

3. Make copies of the Dart Design for half the teams and copies of the Slider Design for the other half, four copies for each team of four.

4. Each student will need a sheet of plain paper, preferably paper that has not been previously used. Half of the teams will need copies of the Dart Design and four 3-cm (about 1.2-in.) pieces of masking tape; the other half of the teams will need copies of the Slider Design.

5. For the contest, students will need to take along their gliders, Part A of the activity sheet, and a pencil. Each team will need a measuring tape. You will need a stopwatch, if you have obtained one, or a watch with a second hand.

Session II

1. You will need to arrange for the same—
    or another—large open space for this
    session as well.

2. Make a copy of Part B of Activity
    Sheet 12 for each student.

3. Have paper clips and masking tape
    handy if students need to use them to
    alter their airplanes.

4. Each student will need his or her glider,
    Part B of the activity sheet, and a
    pencil. Each team will need a
    measuring tape. You will need to take
    along a stopwatch or watch for this
    session.

Background Information

Understanding how an airplane can fly
depends on learning a few basic rules of
aerodynamics, such as how the length,
width, trim, and angle of the wing as well as
the weight of the airplane affect the way an
airplane behaves in the air.

The size of the wing is the most important
factor in determining how an airplane flies.
The "lift" on a wing is the result of the
pressure differential between air passing
over the top and air passing over the bottom
of a wing. Air has to travel farther and faster
over the curved, or cambered, top of a wing
than it does over the flatter bottom part;
and the faster air moves, the lower its
pressure becomes—an example of the
Bernoulli effect. The greater pressure
beneath the wing pushes it—and the
airplane—upward. A large wing displaces
more air than a small wing, and thus
produces more lift.

Viewed from the front, a plane's wings
extend to each side either horizontally
(forming a *T* shape), angle downward
(forming an *A* shape) or angle upward
(forming a *V* shape). The more the wings
angle upward toward a *V* shape, the more
stable the plane will be in the air. However,
the more a wing is angled up, the less it lifts
the plane.

Trim refers to the shape of the rear edge of
the wing. If the rear edge is trimmed, or
bent, that wing will lift that side of the
airplane more. Again, the Bernoulli effect is
evident: air over the top surface of the bent-
down edge must travel even faster to catch
up with air passing over the bottom.
Conversely, if the edge is trimmed upward,
the result is less lift.

On a glider—an airplane without on-board
power—the length of the wingspan
determines how quickly air resistance will
slow it down. A glider with a wide wingspan
has to run through more air in a given
distance than one with a shorter wingspan.
Since it has to push more air aside as it
flies, a glider with wide wings meets more
air resistance and generally slows down
more quickly.

Lastly, the point where the airplane's weight
is concentrated is very important. In this
activity, that point can be determined by
balancing the plane on one finger. If it
balances near the middle of the wing, the
airplane will usually fly well. If the center of
weight is too far in front of the wing, the
airplane will fall over onto its nose. If it is
too far back, the plane will swing up into
the sky and then fall out of the air. The
center of weight can be changed by
attaching a paper clip or a small piece of
masking tape to the end of the plane that is
not heavy enough.

The designs that students will use represent
two proven, but very different, approaches
to flight. One is a small-winged airplane
that will not stay in the air unless it is
traveling fast. It can, however, cover a great
distance in a short time before falling to the
ground. The other has an enormous wing
that allows it to meander slowly through the
air for a long period of time. During this
time, it may either fly straight for a long
distance or fly in circles.

Name _____   Activity Sheet 12, Part A

Paper Airplanes

1. Predict the results of flying either the dart or slider design.

   I think the **dart/slider** (circle one) glider will stay in the air longest because

   Answers will vary.

   _____

   I think the **dart/slider** (circle one) glider will fly farthest because

   Answers will vary.

   _____

2. Record the results of your glider's test flight in the chart below.

Glider Design	Time in the Air	Flight Distance

   Did your test flight prove your prediction? Answers will vary.

3. Record the results of your team's winning glider in the chart below.

Glider Design	Time in the Air	Flight Distance

4. Record the results of the winning gliders in the whole-class contest in the chart below. Write the type of glider and the time or distance in each box in the chart.

	Flight 1	Flight 2	Flight 3
Time in the Air			
Flight Distance			

Name _____   Activity Sheet 12, Part B

Paper Airplanes

5. Make a flight prediction: I will change Answers will vary.

   _____

   on my glider. I think this change will improve its **flight distance/time in the air** (circle one) because

   Answers will vary.

6. Make the change in your glider and flight-test it three times. Record the best of the three results in the chart.

Glider Design	Time in the Air	Flight Distance

   Was your new glider better than your first one? How?
   Answers will vary.

   _____

   What is one feature of a glider that helps it stay in the air a long time? Why?
   A large wing area helps keep it in the air because air resistance increases with area.

   _____

   If a glider is streamlined (dart), will it travel faster or slower through the air than a glider with wide, straight wings (slider)? Why?
   It would travel faster because objects with a long, thin shape run into less air resistance than those with wide, flat shapes.

Teaching Suggestions

Additional Information

Session 1

1 Ask students, **What do you call an airplane that has no engine?**

Some students may know what a glider, or sailplane, is.

Write *glider* on the board. Tell students that today they will construct and fly two kinds of paper airplanes. Since they have no engines, they are called gliders.

Half of the teams will make one type, called the *dart,* and the other teams will make another type, called the *slider.* Write both names on the board.

2 Give each student a copy of Activity Sheet 12, Part A, and a sheet of plain paper.

Divide the class into teams of four. Distribute copies of the Dart Design and four pieces of masking tape to half the teams; distribute copies of the Slider Design to the remaining teams.

Tell all the teams to take a few minutes to study the diagrams and instructions for their gliders before they begin to make them. Tell students that airplanes that are folded carefully fly much better than those that are made quickly and carelessly.

Students in half of the teams will build a dart, a very pointed, narrow airplane with small wings. Students in the other teams will build a slider, a broad-winged airplane with large wings. You may wish to help by demonstrating their construction on an individual, team, or class level.

When they have finished, ask the Dart teams to hold up their gliders so the Slider teams can see them. Then ask the Slider teams to hold up their gliders. Ask students, **Which design do you think will stay in the air the longest? Why do you think so?**

Have them write their names on their finished gliders.

Answers will vary. Encourage speculations based on what students know about air resistance and area.

Ask, **Which design do you think will fly the farthest? Why do you think so?**

Answers will vary. Elicit responses involving air resistance and streamlining.

Have students record their predictions and the reasons for the predictions on Part A of the activity sheet.

3 Tell students that they will enter their planes in a contest to see which design stays in the air for the longest amount of time and which flies the farthest.

Ask students to gather up their gliders, activity sheets, tape measures, and pencils and follow you to the contest area. Take the stopwatch (if you have one).

Upon arriving, explain that as they launch each plane they will count aloud together the number of seconds each plane flies and then measure how far it traveled.

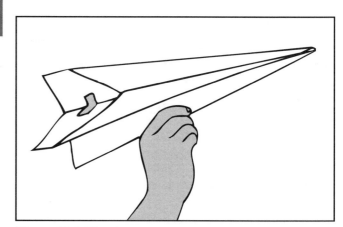

Figure 12-1. The dart.

4 Establish a starting line and have the four members of one team line up behind it, side by side. Tell them that they will launch their planes, one at a time, in the same direction. As soon as they release each plane, time each flight and call out the number of seconds between launch and landing. Have each student write the flight time for his or her glider in the chart in Step 2 on the activity sheet.

If you wish, encourage class participation by leading them in counting the seconds aloud. Students should count "one thousand, two thousand," and so on.

After all four planes have landed, teammates should cooperate in measuring the distances from the starting line to each plane on the ground. Have each student

Students may need your help, depending on the length of the flights, in figuring distances.

record the flight distance for his or her glider in the chart in Step 2 on the activity sheet.

Ask team members to decide which of their planes flew the best. Have them enter the data in the second chart in Step 3 on the activity sheet.

Meanwhile, ask the other students for their opinions on how the planes flew and call the next team up to the flight line.

Continue the flights, one team at a time, until every student has had an opportunity to fly. Then tell each team that they will fly their winning plane in a two-part class competition, one for time and the other for distance.

Figure 12-2. The slider.

After agreeing on a launch method for all entries, have the students who made the top gliders selected by the Dart teams fly their gliders. Time and measure three flights for each entry. Repeat the process with the Slider teams.

Have students record the time and distance data for the winning glider of each type in the chart in Step 4 of the activity sheet. Take students back to the classroom.

Announce which glider had the best performance for time in the air and which glider flew the longest distance from the starting line. Write the results on the board.

A dart will hold the record for the longest distance covered in the shortest amount of time; a slider, however, in its total time in the air, may have covered more distance than a dart. A slider will almost always stay in the air longer than a dart.

Hold up the winning dart and slider gliders and encourage students to compare them and speculate on what differences led to the results. Tell students they will modify their airplanes in the next session to see if they can improve their performance.

Designate an area in the classroom for students to store their planes until the next session. Return the roll of masking tape, the tape measures, and the Dart and Slider masters to the kit.

Give each student a copy of Part B of
Activity Sheet 12 and a pencil. Tell students
that they should now try to improve the
performance of their gliders, increasing either
their time in the air or distance covered.

Write *variable* on the board. Explain that a
variable is a single thing about the glider
that can be changed. Ask, **What variables
can you think of that you might change
to improve your glider's time in the air
or its flight distance?**

*Responses will vary, but elicit suggestions, if
necessary, by asking about changes in shape,
material, size, and so forth.*

Make two lists of students' responses on the
board, one headed *Time in the Air* and the
other *Flight Distance.*

Ask questions to help students relate
suggested changes to what they have
learned about air in previous activities. For
example, ask such questions as the
following:

**Which glider design has the larger wing
area, and how would area affect its
time in the air?**

**If you bent down one side or the other of
the wingtips on a slider, what would
happen to the air pressure on that
side? What would it do to that wing?**

**Would curving down the back edges of a
dart's wingtips speed it up or slow it
down? Keep it in the air longer?**

**What could you do to a dart to keep its
nose from diving down to the ground
too fast?**

**What could you do to a slider to make it
fly straighter?**

*In the class discussion of these and other questions,
use some of the information from this activity's
Background Information, such as the importance of
balancing their planes, to direct the analysis along
helpful lines. For example, show students how to
balance their planes on one finger to find their center
of weight. Tell students to use a paper clip or a piece
of masking tape to add weight to the front or back of
the planes if they think it would improve their
performances.*

Tell students to decide which variable to change on the glider and predict why the change will improve its flight time or distance. Have them enter their predictions and reasons in Step 5 on the activity sheet.

Remind students to change only one variable on their airplane and to leave the rest the same. Give students time to alter their planes. Have paper clips and masking tape handy if students should ask for them.

 Give each team a measuring tape. Tell students to gather up their gliders, activity sheets, and pencils. Take your stopwatch or watch and return with your students to the open testing area. Allow each student three attempts to test the altered plane. Ask his or her teammates to help time and measure each flight.

Have each student record the data for the best flight in the chart in Step 6 on the activity sheet.

After returning to the classroom, ask students to describe the variable they changed and whether it improved their glider's performance. Use their comments to lead a class discussion of which variables had the greatest impact, for better or worse, on the gliders. Encourage students to use this information to create rules on how to design successful gliders.

Tell students to complete Part B of the activity sheet.

Reinforcement

 Give each student a fresh sheet of plain paper and challenge him or her to take some of the elements of the slider and some of the dart and fold a new design of glider with a wingspan somewhere in between the two. Have them test-fly their gliders.

Cleanup

Return the measuring tapes to the kit. If you have used them in Session II, replace the roll of masking tape and the box of small paper clips in the kit. Allow students to take their gliders home if they wish.

Connections

Science Challenge

To demonstrate the importance of controlling all variables in an experiment except the one being tested, help students design and conduct investigations in which two or more variables are changed. For example, students could try to germinate three different types of seeds planted in separate cups and then placed in different locations (sunny, shady, and dark) and watered differently (no water, overwatered, and watered only enough to keep the soil moist) for one week. Discuss students' results, then ask them to explain why those results occurred. Guide them to realize that, without controlling all variables except one, they cannot explain their results with certainty and cannot arrive at valid conclusions.

Science Extension

Provide a variety of age-appropriate source materials so interested students can find out about flying animals, including not only birds but bats, insects, and animals that glide, such as flying frogs, flying squirrels, and flying fish. Encourage each student or team to choose a different type of animal. Give students an opportunity to share their findings in oral reports or bulletin board displays.

Science and Language Arts

Your more capable readers might enjoy reading books about air travel, including *Travel by Air* by Michael Pollard (Schoolhouse Press, 1986). This book covers a wide range of topics, from how airplanes fly to special-purpose planes (such as firefighters and crop-dusters) to planes of the future. In addition to discussing the book's ideas with students in small groups, point out that it is organized into brief chapters, each focusing on a different topic that is identified in the chapter's title. Also review the other parts of the book—the title page, table of contents, glossary, and index—and the function of each.

Science and Social Studies

Encourage interested students to find out about Orville and Wilbur Wright's airplane flight in 1903—the first flight in an aircraft that was, unlike a hot-air balloon, heavier than air and could be fully controlled. The Wright brothers' plane lifted just a few feet into the air, stayed aloft only a few seconds at a top speed of about 48 kilometers per hour (30 mph), and traveled only about 36.5 meters (120 ft). Have students measure off this distance outdoors so they can see how short the flight was.

In December 1986, an ultralight aircraft named *Voyager* flew around the world in 8 days without stopping to refuel. Provide articles from children's magazines and other age-appropriate sources, and encourage your older or more capable students to find out about this flight. Ask them to pay particular attention to the design and construction features that enabled the plane to stay aloft for 8 days without refueling.

Science, Technology, and Society

Have students reexamine the source material you provided for the Science, Technology, and Society activity in Activity 11, this time looking for pictures of "futuristic" airplanes. (Some such planes are shown in *Travel by Air,* cited above.) Are they shaped more like the dart or the slider, or do they have features of both? Comparing them with their own gliders, do students think the futuristic planes are designed to move very quickly or to stay in the air a long time? Why might the planes be designed that way?

Assessment

Objectives

Students are given three different ways to demonstrate their understanding of the material presented in Amazing Air.

The students

- devise, test, and describe a method for shrinking a volume of air

- devise, test, and describe a method for expanding a volume of air

- recognize that a toy with a larger parachute falls more slowly than a toy with a smaller parachute

- identify greater air resistance as the reason the toy with the larger parachute falls more slowly

- describe what happens to tissues in the bottoms of two cups, one cup with a hole in the bottom and one without, when the cups are held upside down underwater

- explain why one tissue gets wet while the other does not, in terms of displacement of air and water

- describe how the shape of a paper airplane affects its performance

- propose an explanation for a balloon expanding on a hot day

- identify air as a substance that takes up space in sealed food bags

- explain the effect of an airstream over a piece of tissue paper, in terms of higher and lower air pressure

Schedule

About 60 minutes; 20 minutes for each section

Materials

For each student

1	Assessment Activity Sheets 1, 2, and 3, Parts A and B
1	*crayon, blue
1	*crayon, yellow
1	*pencil

For the class

8	bases, foam, for syringes
8	*bottles, plastic, with attached balloons (from Activity 4)
1 stick	clay, modeling
8	containers, plastic, 6-L
8	*containers, 2-L or greater
	*ice cubes
	*newspaper
8	*syringes, with clay plugs (from Activity 5)
24	*textbooks, hardcover
	*water, tap, cold
	*water, tap, hot

*provided by the teacher

Preparation

1. Make a copy of Assessment Activity Sheets 1, 2, and 3, Parts A and B, for each student. Make one copy of the Assessment Summary Chart for the class.

2. Check to see that the balloons still form a tight seal on the necks of the bottles, without any air leaks.

3. Check to see that the clay balls still form a seal in the tips of the syringes. Adjust as needed to form the seal, as described in the Preparation section of Activity 5.

4. Fill eight of the containers with cold tap water and add ice cubes to each. Fill the other eight containers with hot tap water.

5. Cover each of the eight hands-on stations with several sheets of newspaper to catch spills. At each hands-on station, place one container of ice water, one container of hot tap water, one sealed syringe, one foam syringe base, one bottle with balloon over the neck, and three textbooks.

6. Plan how to divide the class into three groups. Group one will start at the hands-on stations. Groups two and three will need desks or tables at which to work. Students in group two will need a blue crayon and a yellow crayon. Every student will need a pencil.

Background Information

This multi-dimensional assessment is designed to measure students' understanding more thoroughly than traditional tests. Section 1 assesses students' proficiency through hands-on tasks; Section 2, through picture interpretation; and Section 3, through verbal questions.

Assessment Instructions

Tell students that the purpose of the upcoming activities is to provide three ways to assess some of what they have learned from the module.

1

Divide the class into three groups. Assign one group Section 1 of the assessment; the second group, Section 2; and the third group, Section 3. (If more than eight students are in a group, some students will have to perform the hands-on portion of the assessment after the other groups have finished.) Distribute the appropriate activity sheets to each group. Tell the students that all the materials they need to complete Section 1 are at the hands-on stations.

Have students participating in Section 1 move to the prepared hands-on stations. Have students in groups two and three sit at their desks and await instructions.

Give oral instructions to group one first. Tell them that their task for Assessment Activity Sheet 1, Part A, is to figure out a method to shrink a volume of air, using the materials provided at the stations. Tell them that they should first think of a method, then test their method to make sure it works, then draw a picture of their method in the space provided. Finally, they need to describe their method and explain why it works. For Part B, they need to figure out a method for expanding a volume of air, test it, draw a picture, and explain why the method works.

Give oral instructions to group two. Tell them that their task is to read Assessment Activity Sheet 2, Parts A and B, and follow the instructions. Depending on the reading level of your students, you may wish to read the items out loud and answer any questions your students may have.

Give oral instructions to group three. Tell students to read and answer the questions. Depending on the reading level of your students, you may wish to read the items out loud and answer any questions your students may have.

Name _____ Assessment Activity Sheet 1, Part A

Assessment – Section 1

1. Look at the materials at your station. Think of a way to shrink a volume of air using the materials you see.

2. Test your way of shrinking a volume of air.

3. Draw a picture of your setup below. Tell how your setup shrinks the volume of air.

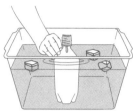

Answers will vary. Students may have used books to press on air in the syringe, which shrinks its volume, as shown above left. Students may have put the balloon and bottle setup into cold water, as shown above right. This method decreases the temperature of the air, making the air take up less space. Students may have pushed the plunger by hand, or pushed the balloon into the bottle by hand. Students may have even tried putting the sealed syringe into cold water.

Name _____ Assessment Activity Sheet 1, Part B

Assessment – Section 1

1. Look at the materials at your station. Think of a way to expand a volume of air, using the materials you see.

2. Test your way of expanding a volume of air.

3. Draw a picture of your setup below. Tell how your setup expands the volume of air.

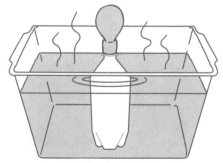

Answers will vary. Students may have put the balloon and bottle setup into hot water. This method increases the temperature of the air, which makes the air take up more space as shown above. Students may also have pulled on the plunger of the syringe to make the air take more space. Student may have even tried putting the sealed syringe into hot water.

Assessment – Section 2

Michael and Rufus are having a contest designing parachutes for their toy mice. The mouse that takes the longest to fall to the ground wins the contest. The two mice in their parachutes are shown below.

Michael's mouse   **Rufus's mouse**

Which mouse will win the contest? Why?

<u>Rufus's mouse will win because it has a larger</u>
<u>parachute.</u>

How does the size of the parachute affect who wins the contest? (*Hint:* Use the term *air resistance* in your answer.)

<u>The air resistance is greater against the larger</u>
<u>parachute, so it takes longer to fall.</u>

Assessment – Section 2

Mitra has two cups. One cup has a hole in the bottom. The other cup does not have a hole. Mitra stuffs a tissue into the bottom of each cup. She turns the cups upside down and pushes them into the water, as shown in the picture.

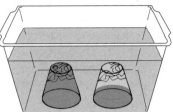

Does water enter both cups?

<u>Water enters one cup but not the other.</u>

Color each cup to show what is inside. Color the water blue. Color the air yellow. (Do not color the water in the container.)

What happens to the tissue in each cup?

<u>The tissue in the cup with the hole will get wet. The</u>
<u>tissue in the cup without the hole will stay dry.</u>

Why does the tissue in one cup get wet, while the other stays dry?

<u>The air escapes from the cup with the hole, so the</u>
<u>water has room to enter the cup and wet the</u>
<u>tissue. The cup without the hole does not give the</u>
<u>air anywhere to go, so water cannot enter the cup.</u>

Assessment – Section 3

1. Emma's cousin suggests they make paper airplanes and see which one is better. First, Emma wants to know what "better" means. Does the "better" airplane fly the farthest distance, or does it stay in the air the longest time? Her cousin says it makes no difference. Emma says yes, it does! Why does Emma want to know what "better" means before she makes her airplane? Explain how the design of the airplane affects how it moves in the air.

<u>Emma will use a narrow design if "better" means</u>
<u>"flies farther." This design decreases air</u>
<u>resistance, and allows the plane to fly farther.</u>
<u>She will use a wide design if "better" means</u>
<u>"stays in the air longer." This design increases air</u>
<u>resistance, allowing the plane to stay aloft longer.</u>

2. Kevin buys a balloon at the mall. The mall is air-conditioned and cool. Kevin leaves the mall and walks home with his balloon. It is summer, and it is hot outside. He has a long walk and, on the way home, he notices that his balloon looks bigger than it did in the mall, and its skin looks stretched more tightly. Explain how going from a cool building to the hot outdoors could make the balloon bigger and stretched more tightly. (*Hint:* How is air volume affected by temperature?)

<u>The balloon is filled up with air inside the cool</u>
<u>building. When Kevin takes the balloon outdoors,</u>
<u>the temperature of the air in the balloon rises.</u>
<u>When its temperature rises, the air expands and</u>
<u>takes up more space. As a result, the skin of the</u>
<u>balloon stretches to hold the larger volume.</u>

Assessment – Section 3

3. Tai and Lu are putting trail mix into airtight, reclosable bags for a scout hike. Tai is pushing most of the air out of the bags before closing them. Lu is leaving a lot of air in the bags as he closes them. Both boys make ten bags. Tai's ten bags all fit in one box. Lu's ten bags do not fit in one box, even though they have the same amount of trail mix as Tai's bags. Explain why Tai's bags fit, but Lu's do not. Then tell how Lu could make his bags fit.

<u>Lu's bags have more air in them than Tai's. Air</u>
<u>takes up space, so Lu's bags take up more space.</u>
<u>Lu could open his bags and squeeze the air out</u>
<u>before reclosing them. Or, Lu could try to use</u>
<u>high pressure or low temperature to make his</u>
<u>bags fit in a smaller space (but these methods</u>
<u>would be much harder to do).</u>

4. Liza blows across the top of a sheet of tissue paper. The tissue paper rises up as she blows. It falls down again when she stops. Is the air pressure high or low across the top of the paper while she is blowing? How do you know?

<u>The air pressure across the top of the paper is</u>
<u>low while she is blowing. Low air pressure pulls,</u>
<u>while high air pressure pushes. Her blowing</u>
<u>makes low air pressure that pulls the paper up.</u>

When all groups have finished, collect the assessment activity sheets from each group and rotate the groups. At the hands-on stations, check the temperature of the hot and cold water baths and add ice cubes and replace the hot tap water, as needed. Assign Assessment Section 1 to group two, Section 2 to group three, and Section 3 to group one. Have group two trade places with group one at the hands-on stations. Distribute the appropriate activity sheets to each group.

Repeat this rotation one last time so that all groups complete each section of the assessment.

Scoring

Answers are printed on the reduced assessment activity sheets on the preceding pages. However, in some cases, various answers are appropriate. An example of a reasonable answer for each open-ended question is given, but students may think of other, equally appropriate responses.

The Assessment Summary Chart allows you to summarize class and individuals' mastery of skills and concepts, and to show parents or principals the students' accomplishments.

Scoring Key for Assessment Summary Chart

○ not appropriate or gave no answer

✓ appropriate but gave one or more incorrect answers

● appropriate and gave no incorrect answer(s)

For each student, one of the above symbols should be entered in each column of the Assessment Summary Chart.

Glossary

air The mixture of gases that surrounds the earth's surface.

air pressure The force with which a body of air pushes in all directions.

air resistance The resistance felt by an object moving through air as it collides with air molecules; resistance increases as the size and speed of the object increases.

area The amount of two-dimensional space occupied by an object.

balance A device used to determine the weight of an object, or to compare the weights of two different objects.

barometer A device that measures the pressure of the air around us.

Bernoulli effect The law that describes how a stream of air passing through a narrow space experiences a decrease in pressure.

conserved Maintained constant or unchanged.

control The part of an experiment in which all variables are held constant; the control is later compared with other parts of the experiment in which variables have been changed.

cubic centimeter (cc) A metric unit of measure for volume.

displace To move into the space formerly occupied by another substance.

glider An aircraft that does not provide its own power to stay in the air.

graduated cylinder A cylindrical container marked in units for measuring the volume of the contents.

parachute A device that uses a large area of lightweight material to increase air resistance as it falls through the air, thus slowing the descent of the person or object suspended from it.

prediction A guess, based on experience, about what will probably happen in a certain situation.

pressure The application of force on an object by something in contact with it.

properties The characteristics of something by which it can be described.

streamlined Referring to the shape of an object that is usually narrowed and tapered so as to reduce air resistance to its forward movement.

temperature The measurement of the hotness or coldness of a substance.

thermometer A heat-sensitive device used to measure temperature in units of degrees on a scale.

variable A factor in an experiment that can be deliberately changed in order to find out what results from the change. (Compare with *control.*)

volume The amount of space taken up by something.

wind The movement of higher-pressure air toward lower-pressure air.

wind speed indicator A device used to measure the speed of wind.

References and Resources

Air
Michael Allaby. Facts on File, 1992.

Air
Kitty Benedict. Creative Education, 1992.

Air
Su Swallow. Watts, 1991.

Air, Air All Around
Joanne Barkan. Silver Press, 1990.

Air, Air Everywhere
Tom Johnston. Gareth Stevens, 1988.

Air: All about Cyclones, Rainbows, Clouds, Ozone and More
David Allen. Firefly, 1993.

Air and Flying
Barbara Taylor. Watts, 1991.

The Air I Breathe
Bobbie Kalman and Janine Schaub. Crabtree, 1993.

Air: Simple Experiments for Young Scientists
Larry White. Millbrook Press, 1995.

Airplanes and Flying Machines
Jeunesse Gallimard. Scholastic, 1992.

Balloon Ride
Evelyn Clarke Mott. Walker, 1991.

Experiments with Air
Ray Broekel. Children's Press, 1988.

Flying Machines
Norman Barrett. Watts, 1994.

Planes
Francesca Baines. Watts, 1995.

Planes, Gliders, Helicopters and Other Flying Machines
Terry Jennings. Larousse Kingfisher Chambers, 1993.

The Science Book of Air
Neil Ardley. Harcourt Brace Jovanovich, 1991.

Science with Air
Helen Edom and Moira Butterfield. Usborne, 1991.

Simple Science Projects with Air
John Williams. Gareth Stevens, 1992.

States of Matter
Delta Education. Delta Education, Inc., 1996.

Weather Watching
Delta Education. Delta Education, Inc., 1996.

What Will the Weather Be?
Lynda DeWitt. HarperCollins, 1993.

Air Is Something

1. Blow up your plastic bag until it is full and tie it shut.

What is inside the bag? _____

2. In the pictures below, draw the balloon as it looked on the end of the syringe with the plunger pushed in; then draw it as it looked with the plunger pulled out.

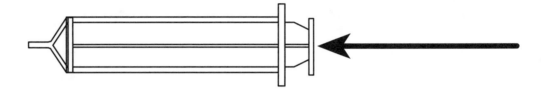

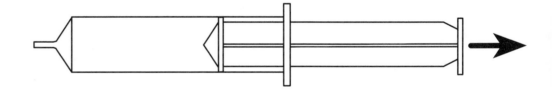

3. In each picture above, color the place where air is.

Did the air move when you pulled back the plunger to the end of the syringe? If so, where did it come from, and where did it go?

_____

_____

_____

Air Is Something

4. With your teammates, connect the two syringes with the piece of tubing, as shown below.

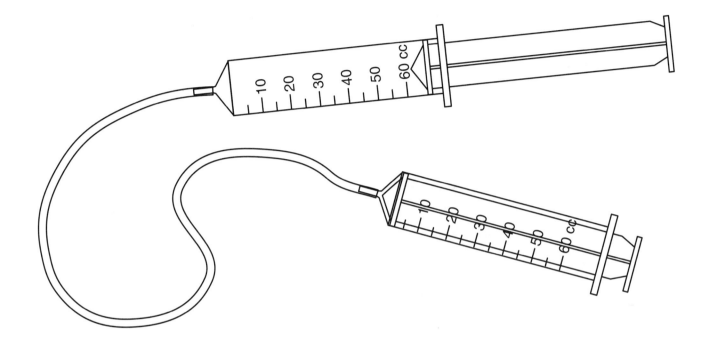

5. In the picture above, color in the place where air is.

What happened when you pushed in the plunger of one syringe?

_____

_____

_____

Why did the second plunger move out in its syringe when you pushed in the plunger of the first syringe?

_____

_____

_____

Air Takes Up Space

1. Record your prediction:

What do you think will happen to the paper towel when the cup is placed under water?

_____

What did you observe about the paper towel after the cup was removed from the water?

_____

2. Complete Part B of Activity Sheet 2. Then come back and finish this sheet.

What do you think will happen to the paper towel when the cup with the hole in it is turned upside down and pushed under water?

_____

_____

What did you observe about the paper towel when the cup was removed from the water?

_____

_____

How do you explain this?

_____

_____

Air Takes Up Space

3. With your teammates, construct the setup shown below.

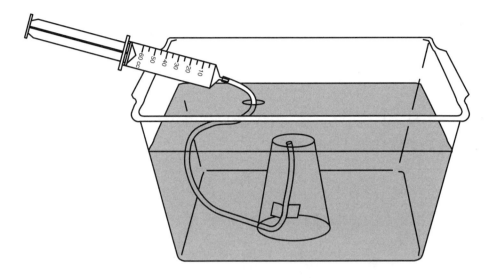

What do you think will happen when you push in the plunger?

_____

What happened when you pushed in the plunger?

_____

4. Take your cup out of the water. Remove the syringe and place your finger over the end of the tubing. Push the cup upside down to the bottom of the container.

What do you think will happen if you remove your finger from the end of the tubing?

_____

What happened when you removed your finger from the end of the tubing?

_____

Why was the water able to displace the air in the cup?

_____

Air Has Volume

Before Pouring:

1. In the picture, color the space where water is.

What is the volume of water in the first cylinder?

_____

In the second cylinder?

_____

What is the total volume of water in the first and second cylinders?

_____

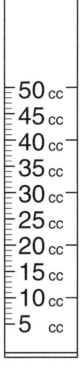

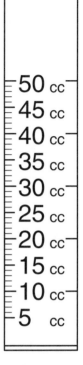

cylinder 1   **cylinder 2**

After pouring:

2. In each picture, color the space where water is.

What is the volume of water in the first cylinder?

_____

In the second cylinder?

_____

What is the total volume of water in the first and second cylinders?

_____

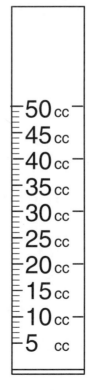

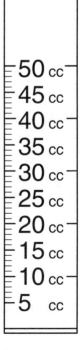

cylinder 1   **cylinder 2**

Air Has Volume

3. Predict: What do you think will happen if you split a volume of air into two parts? Will the volume be conserved?

_____

_____

4. With your teammates, construct the setup shown below.

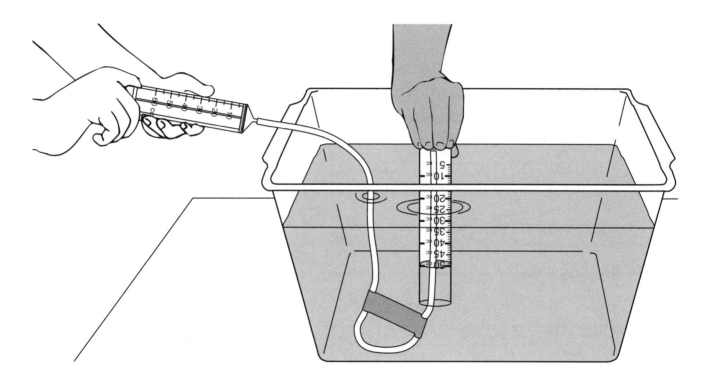

Before transferring the air:

What is the volume of the air in the first cylinder? _____

After transferring the air:

What is the volume of air in the first cylinder? _____

What is the volume of air in the second cylinder? _____

What is the total volume of air in the first and second cylinders? _____

Is the volume of air conserved when it is divided? _____

Air Volume and Temperature

1. Record the temperatures outside the bottle.

Air temperature _____

Water temperature _____

2. After you have placed the balloon over the neck of your bottle, draw the way your balloon looks on the bottle in the picture to the right.

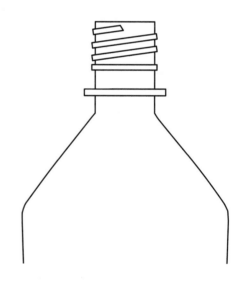

3. Record the temperature inside the bottle every 30 seconds for 3 minutes. Your teacher will call out the times listed below. Write the number of degrees on your thermometer on the line opposite the time.

Start _____	1:30 _____	3:00 _____
0:30 _____	2:00 _____	
1:00 _____	2:30 _____	

Air Volume and Temperature

4. On the picture of the bottle to the right, draw the way your balloon looks after the bottle has been in the container of water for 3 minutes. Write *hot water* or *cold water* under the bottle, depending on which one your team used.

What happened to the balloon?

_____

_____

_____

_____

What is the relationship between temperature and volume?

_____

_____

_____

Air Volume and Pressure

1. Look at your team's syringe and read the number closest to the bottom of the plunger.

What is the volume of air inside the syringe? _____

2. You will be placing books on top of the plunger one at a time and reading the volume of air in the syringe each time. In the chart below, record what you predict the volume will be when you add another book; then, after you add the book, record the volume in cc that you observe.

Number of Books	Prediction	Result
0		
1		
2		
3		
4		

What is the relationship between pressure and volume?

_____

_____

_____

Does Air Have Weight?

Do you think air has weight?

_____

Assemble your balance as shown below.

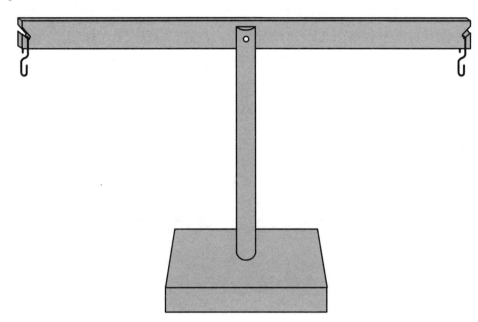

In what position is the balance beam when the objects on either side weigh the same?

_____

In what position is the balance beam when the objects on either side do not weigh the same?

_____

_____

When you put an empty balloon on one side of the beam and an inflated balloon on the other, which side went down?

_____

What can you conclude about air from your experiment?

_____

_____

Air Exerts Pressure

1. With your teammates, assemble your barometer. First, study the labeled illustration. Then, follow the instructions below, step by step.

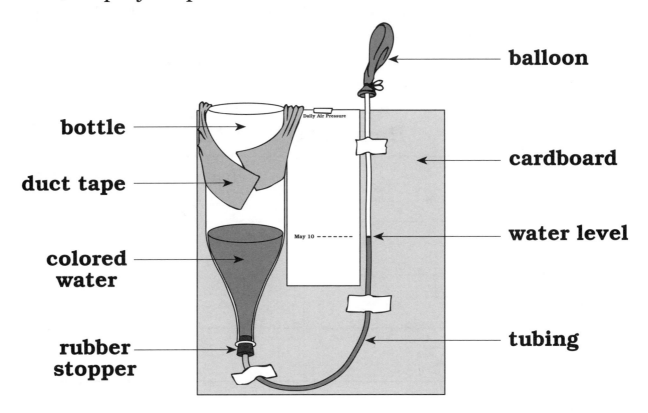

- Insert the stopper with tubing firmly into the bottle of colored water.

- Tape the Daily Air Pressure sheet to the top center of the cardboard.

- Hold up the tubing, turn the bottle upside down, and tape it to the cardboard.

- Loop up the tubing and tape it to the cardboard in three places.

- Tie the balloon onto the free end of the tubing with a rubber band.

- Mark the water level in the tubing on the measuring sheet and add today's date.

Air Exerts Pressure

2. Record your team's barometer data in the chart below. In the first column, write the date each time you check the level of the colored water in the tubing. In the second column, draw an up-arrow (↑) if the water level is above the last dotted line you drew, a down-arrow (↓) if the water level is below the last dotted line, and a horizontal arrow (→) if the water level is even with the last dotted line.

Barometer Data	
Date	**Barometer Reading** ↑, ↓, or →

What conclusion did you and your teammates reach after recording the water level in your barometer for a number of days?

_____

_____

High Pressure—Low Pressure

Predict:

1. What do you think will happen to the water level in the tubing when you push down on the balloon?

_____

2. Push on the balloon and observe what happens to the water level in the tubing. Draw the water level in the tubing in the appropriate cup below.

Predict:

3. What do you think will happen to the water level in the tubing when you pull up on the balloon?

_____

4. Pull up on the balloon and observe what happens to the water level in the tubing. Draw the water level in the tubing in the appropriate cup below.

What does high air pressure do to other materials?

_____

What does low air pressure do to other materials?

_____

Air Resistance

1. Follow the directions below to make your parachute.

- Knot the four strings together at one end.

- Make a small loop at the other end of each string and stick it onto a piece of tape.

- Open the bag and tape the strings to its outside edge, spacing the strings evenly.

- Attach the washer to the knotted end of the strings.

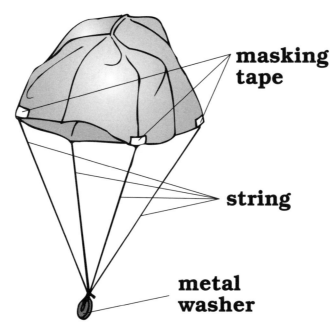

masking tape

string

metal washer

When you and your teammate dropped the plain washer and the washer on the parachute from the same height above the floor and at the same time, what did you observe?

_____

_____

How does a parachute use air to slow down a falling object attached to it?

_____

_____

Air Resistance

2. Work together with your teammate to attach the rubber bands to the washer on your parachute. Look at the illustrations and follow the directions below.

- Hold one of the rubber bands and put the second one halfway through it.

- Put one loop of the second band through its other loop and pull it taut.

- Join the washer to one of the rubber bands in the same manner.

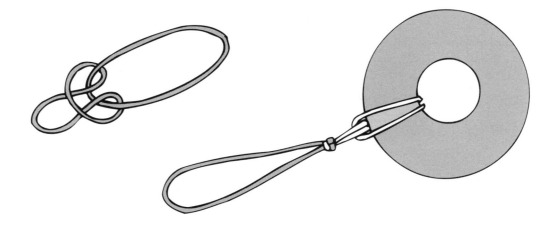

When you walked and then ran with your parachute, what happened to the rubber bands?

_____

_____

_____

As an object moves through air faster and faster, does the air offer more or less resistance to the object? (Use the term *air resistance* in your answer.)

_____

_____

Air Moves

1. Follow your teacher's directions and make the wind speed indicator shown in the picture.

2. Predict which location in the school yard will be the windiest today.

_____

_____

_____

_____

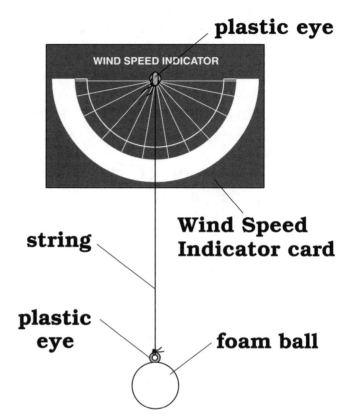

plastic eye

WIND SPEED INDICATOR

Wind Speed Indicator card

string

plastic eye

foam ball

3. Following your outdoor measurements, record your results in the chart below.

	Location	Highest Wind Speed in m.p.h.
1.		
2.		
3.		

Why does wind speed differ from one place to another?

_____

_____

_____

The Bernoulli Effect

1. Follow your teacher's directions and attach the foam balls to the flaps on the trapezoid piece as pictured below.

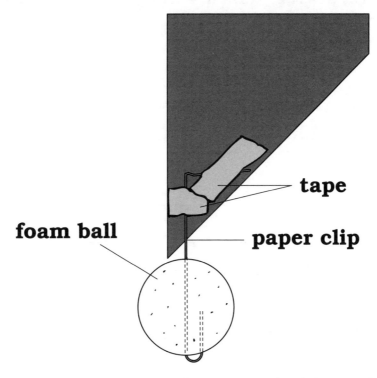

tape

foam ball   **paper clip**

2. Predict: What will happen when you hold up the device and blow hard through the space between the two foam balls?

_____

_____

What happened to the foam balls when you blew into the space between them? Why did it happen?

_____

_____

_____

3. Describe the Bernoulli effect.

_____

_____

Paper Airplanes

1. Predict the results of flying either the dart or slider design.

   I think the **dart/slider** (circle one) glider will stay in the air longest because

   _____

   _____

   I think the **dart/slider** (circle one) glider will fly farthest because

   _____

   _____

2. Record the results of your glider's test flight in the chart below.

Glider Design	Time in the Air	Flight Distance

   Did your test flight prove your prediction? _____

3. Record the results of your team's winning glider in the chart below.

Glider Design	Time in the Air	Flight Distance

4. Record the results of the winning gliders in the whole-class contest in the chart below. Write the type of glider and the time or distance in each box in the chart.

	Flight 1	Flight 2	Flight 3
Time in the Air			
Flight Distance			

Paper Airplanes

5. Make a flight prediction: I will change _____

_____

on my glider. I think this change will improve its
flight distance/time in the air (circle one) because

_____

_____

6. Make the change in your glider and flight-test it three
times. Record the best of the three results in the chart.

Glider Design	Time in the Air	Flight Distance

Was your new glider better than your first one? How?

_____

_____

What is one feature of a glider that helps it stay in the air a
long time? Why?

_____

_____

If a glider is streamlined (dart), will it travel faster or slower
through the air than a glider with wide, straight wings
(slider)? Why?

_____

_____

Assessment – Section 1

1. Look at the materials at your station. Think of a way to shrink a volume of air using the materials you see.

2. Test your way of shrinking a volume of air.

3. Draw a picture of your setup below. Tell how your setup shrinks the volume of air.

_____

_____

_____

_____

_____

_____

_____

_____

_____

Assessment – Section 1

1. Look at the materials at your station. Think of a way to expand a volume of air, using the materials you see.

2. Test your way of expanding a volume of air.

3. Draw a picture of your setup below. Tell how your setup expands the volume of air.

_____

_____

_____

_____

_____

_____

Assessment – Section 2

Michael and Rufus are having a contest designing parachutes for their toy mice. The mouse that takes the longest to fall to the ground wins the contest. The two mice in their parachutes are shown below.

Michael's mouse

Rufus's mouse

Which mouse will win the contest? Why?

_____

_____

_____

How does the size of the parachute affect who wins the contest? (*Hint:* Use the term *air resistance* in your answer.)

_____

_____

Assessment – Section 2

Mitra has two cups. One cup has a hole in the bottom. The other cup does not have a hole. Mitra stuffs a tissue into the bottom of each cup. She turns the cups upside down and pushes them into the water, as shown in the picture.

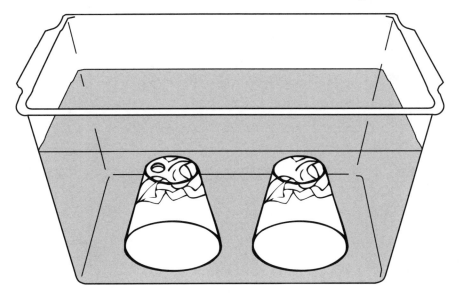

Does water enter both cups?

_____

Color each cup to show what is inside. Color the water blue. Color the air yellow. (Do not color the water in the container.)

What happens to the tissue in each cup?

_____

_____

Why does the tissue in one cup get wet, while the other stays dry?

_____

_____

_____

Assessment – Section 3

1. Emma's cousin suggests they make paper airplanes and see which one is better. First, Emma wants to know what "better" means. Does the "better" airplane fly the farthest distance, or does it stay in the air the longest time? Her cousin says it makes no difference. Emma says yes, it does! Why does Emma want to know what "better" means before she makes her airplane? Explain how the design of the airplane affects how it moves in the air.

_____

_____

_____

_____

_____

2. Kevin buys a balloon at the mall. The mall is air-conditioned and cool. Kevin leaves the mall and walks home with his balloon. It is summer, and it is hot outside. He has a long walk and, on the way home, he notices that his balloon looks bigger than it did in the mall, and its skin looks stretched more tightly. Explain how going from a cool building to the hot outdoors could make the balloon bigger and stretched more tightly. (*Hint:* How is air volume affected by temperature?)

_____

_____

_____

_____

Assessment – Section 3

3. Tai and Lu are putting trail mix into airtight, reclosable bags for a scout hike. Tai is pushing most of the air out of the bags before closing them. Lu is leaving a lot of air in the bags as he closes them. Both boys make ten bags. Tai's ten bags all fit in one box. Lu's ten bags do not fit in one box, even though they have the same amount of trail mix as Tai's bags. Explain why Tai's bags fit, but Lu's do not. Then tell how Lu could make his bags fit.

_____

_____

_____

_____

_____

_____

4. Liza blows across the top of a sheet of tissue paper. The tissue paper rises up as she blows. It falls down again when she stops. Is the air pressure high or low across the top of the paper while she is blowing? How do you know?

_____

_____

_____

_____

Assessment Summary Chart

Name	Section 1		Section 2					Section 3			
	• devised, tested, and described a method for shrinking a volume of air	• devised, tested, and described a method for expanding a volume of air	• recognized that a toy with a larger parachute falls more slowly than a toy with a smaller parachute	• identified greater air resistance as the reason the toy with the larger parachute fell more slowly	• described what happened to tissues in the bottoms of two cups, one cup with a hole in the bottom and one without, when the cups were held upside down underwater	• explained why one tissue got wet while the other did not, in terms of displacement of air and water	• described how the shape of a paper airplane affected its performance	• proposed an explanation for a balloon expanding on a hot day	• identified air as a substance that takes up space in sealed food bags	• explained the effect of an airstream over a piece of tissue paper, in terms of higher and lower air pressure